Sock and Mi ~~~~~~~~~~~~~~~~~~~~~~~~~~~~~~ t-tens. Now you can use them to make a whole theater of fabulous puppets for little people eight months and up.

Magnetic Cars and Raceway—Combining the lure of race cars with the magic of magnets, this game for five-year-olds teaches basic physics and improves eye-hand coordination.

Can You Find Me?—For the littlest tots and toddlers, there's nothing more fascinating than you and the sound of your voice as they learn to listen and follow visual clues.

Blow and Go—Who hasn't blown the wrapper of a straw across the room? These activities let preschool and kindergarten kids see the power of the puff . . . and learn about measuring without it feeling like school.

Little Me—Take some of your child's outgrown clothes, a baby-size doll or Teddy bear, and you can make a personalized keepsake you and your child will treasure.

Will It Float?—All you need is a bowl, basin, or a kid in a bathtub and you can teach basic physics. Some challenging variations for older kids make this a science project bonanza!

Seashell Wind Chime—No child can resist collecting shells at the beach. Add a piece of driftwood, some fishing line, and ribbon, and he can feel like a professional crafter.

AND MASTER THE MOST IMPORTANT LESSON OF ALL—HOW TO HAVE FUN *TOGETHER*

Parents Picks

THE
ACTIVITY
BOOK

More Than 300 Kid-Pleasing,
Skill-Building, Entertaining Activities
for Children from Birth to Age 8

By Marge Kennedy, Karen White,
and the Editors of *Parents* Magazine

St. Martin's Paperbacks

An earlier edition was published under the title *Parents Play and Learn*.

THE ACTIVITY BOOK

Copyright © 2000 by Roundtable Press, Inc., and G + J USA Publishing.

Cover photograph © Penny Gentieu.

Library of Congress Catalog Card Number: 99-23467

ISBN: 0-312-98874-5

Printed in the United States of America

St. Martin's Press Griffin edition / March 2000
St. Martin's Paperbacks edition / October 2003

St. Martin's Paperbacks are published by St. Martin's Press, 175 Fifth Avenue, New York, NY 10010.

10   9   8   7   6   5   4   3   2   1

CONTENTS

• • •

each chapter is organized chronologically by age

FOREWORD

Dear Parents,

In our overscheduled, computer-happy, pop-in-a-video lives, we often forget about the simple games and projects that make kids happy. This book, written especially for busy parents, is filled with hundreds of quick, can-do ideas that not only entertain babies and young children but actually teach them lifelong skills. For instance, do you realize that when you're mixing paints, you're demonstrating the concepts of chemistry, and something as simple as a game of hopscotch builds aiming, jumping, and thinking skills?

But *The Activity Book* isn't just filled with activities; it also teaches important parenting skills. *You* are your child's first—and favorite—teacher. But you can also learn from him. While you hopefully already know how to toss a ball or bang a drum, we think that every adult can benefit from a refresher course in play. Watch your child's face as you're singing a song, building a rocket, searching for shadows, or just sharing a giggle. If your smile is as wide as his, you've mastered the most important lesson of all—how to have fun.

Sally Lee
Editor-in-Chief

INTRODUCTION

These are exciting times in your relationship with your child. As your child's first teacher, you'll help her develop her body, her mind, her sense of herself, and her place in the world. After your child has begun her formal education, you'll be called on to enhance and extend the learning that takes place in the classroom.

To help you make the most of your time with your child, we've put together over three hundred activities that promote your child's learning in every way—ideas for homemade crafts and games that are just right for your child's growing skills. There are physical activities that hone your child's abilities to use her senses and her body; quiet games that increase her cognitive skills; activities that involve her in the natural world; and ideas for excursions that allow your child to stretch her growing abilities around the neighborhood and on her travels.

In gathering the material for this book, we turned to teachers in child-care centers, nursery schools, kindergartens, and elementary schools to observe their work and to gain insights into the many ways in which children learn. We spoke to many parents of newborns and children through the early school years and observed their playful interactions with their children. And we talked to the kids, too, to get their best ideas on learning and having fun. Of course, readers of *Parents* magazine also provided many of the great ideas for playtime activities included in this book.

We hope these ideas will enrich your time with your child, adding another level of fun and learning to your daily interactions.

at-home fun

crafts and games made from household items

In this section of *The Activity Book*, you'll find ways to transform everyday household items into toys and arts-and-crafts projects that will educate and entertain your child for hours. None of these projects requires expensive materials or much preparation time, but all promise to make the minutes and hours you spend playing together more rewarding—and more fun.

at-home fun

Basic arts-and-crafts tools

In addition to a safe, well-lit workstation that includes a table and comfortable chair, your child over the age of 3 needs:

- Crayons, washable markers, finger-paints, and water paints
- Paintbrushes in a variety of sizes
- A variety of paper and cardboard, including plain white paper, construction paper, poster board, paper plates and cups, and tissue paper
- Tape and white glue or paste
- Safety scissors, one-hole punch, and ruler
- Storage containers to organize his or her art materials

Household objects, tools, and materials

These items, some of which are not appropriate for young children to use on their own, can be part of your at-home supplies, too.

- Pens, permanent markers, and glitter
- Recyclables, such as plastic containers and bottles, polystyrene, fabric swatches, cardboard tubes and boxes, used white paper, and wood scraps
- Masking tape and double-sided tape
- Stapler and staples, paper clips, paper fasteners, rubber bands, and pushpins
- Scissors, wire cutters, craft and utility knives, and sharp kitchen knives

Recipes for arts-and-crafts supplies
Play Clay

In a bowl, combine 6 cups of flour, 3 cups of salt, and 3 tablespoons of powdered alum (available in the baking section of the supermarket). Mix well. Add 6 cups of boiling water and stir well. When cool, pour the mixture onto wax paper, and add 1 tablespoon of corn oil or other cooking oil to the mound, covering it completely. Divide it into four sections and knead one section at a time for 7 to 10 minutes. Add a different food coloring to each batch until the dough is well blended and the color is even. Store each batch in a plastic bag in the refrigerator.

Finger-Paint

Commercially produced finger-paints are superior to this homemade variety, but this recipe can provide an inexpensive alternative. Mix ¼ cup of liquid laundry starch with 2 drops of food coloring. Make a separate batch for each color. Store in a closed contained in the refrigerator.

Poster Paint

In a saucepan, slowly add 1 cup of water to ¼ cup of flour. Heat the mixture, stirring constantly, for about 3 minutes. When it begins to thicken, remove it from the burner. Let cool. Then add 2 tablespoons of dry paint (available at art-supply stores) and 2 tablespoons of water. For glossy paint, add ½ teaspoon of liquid dish detergent. Stir. Store in jars with tightly fitted lids.

Papier-Mâché

You can purchase papier-mâché mix at an art-supply store or make your own with a combination of flour and water. You'll also need newspaper, cut into strips about 1" × 4". Many papier-mâché objects are molded around a latex balloon, which can pose a choking hazard. Therefore, papier-mâché work with balloons must be thoroughly supervised.

Bubble Mix
Mix 1 quart of water with about 2 ounces of baby shampoo or dish detergent and 2 ounces of glycerin, available at the drugstore.

My Life Story

Looking over one's life—even the first few very exciting months of it—is an activity that will grow in meaning for your child. When selecting a photo album for your infant, choose one that holds photos only; for toddlers and preschoolers opt for one with self-adhesive pages that can hold both photos and sheets of paper.

ages: 6 months and up
prep time: about 30 minutes **skills:** • visual   discrimination • listening • storytelling

what you need
- Photos of your child and other important people in her life
- Plastic-page photo album
- Plain or colored paper
- Paper memorabilia (optional)

what to do
For infants
1. Choose about six portrait shots that clearly show the faces of people who are familiar to your child.
2. Place the photos in the plastic-encased sleeves of the album.
3. Review the photos with your baby, talking about the dif-

ferent people shown. Encourage her to interact with the pictures, touching them and giving them kisses. Add new photos every few weeks to hold his interest.

For toddlers and preschoolers

1. With your child's help, collect photos of your child, family members, playmates, home, room, and places that are important to her in the neighborhood, such as her preschool and favorite playground.
2. Place the photos on the self-adhesive pages of the album.
3. Have your child dictate something important to her about each picture and transcribe what she says on a piece of paper. Place this dictation in the album as a caption to the photo.
4. Keep this special book with her other favorite reading material to be read again and again.

---

extra!

Create special books for special occasions. For instance:

- A memory book of a vacation or a birthday party, so she can relive the experience. Include postcards, notecards, or similar paper memorabilia, too.

- A preview book, showing photos of not-too-familiar relatives, so she can get to know them before a planned meeting or reunion.

- A book that details a typical day—waking up, getting dressed, eating breakfast—right through bedtime. Reading this can be a comforting finish to any day.

Maracas

A love of rhythm and a few items from the kitchen are all you need to make maracas. Choose containers that are small enough for your child to handle, such as small yogurt containers. Clear plastic soda bottles, with labels removed, also work well and provide the added benefit of letting your child see what's inside.

ages: 8 months and up
prep time: about 5 minutes
skills: • manual dexterity • understanding sound patterns

what you need
- Plastic containers (6- to 8-oz. size) with tight-fitting lids
- ¼ cup dried beans, peas, pasta, or rice
- Heavy-duty tape

what to do
1. Thoroughly wash and dry the containers.
2. Fill each about 1/3 full with dried beans or other noisemakers.
3. Secure the lids with heavy-duty tape.

In addition to enjoying the noise she can make on her own, your child (over the age of 14 months or so) will have fun playing a simple mimicking game that you initiate. You'll need your own maraca for this. To play, shake your maraca twice and invite her to shake hers twice. Then shake yours three times and ask her to do the same. Work out a number of different sound patterns and let her take a turn playing bandleader.

Sock and Mitten People

There's no need to throw out stray socks or mittens. Now you can use them to make a whole theater full of fabulous puppets.

ages: 8 months and up

prep time:
about 5 to 10 minutes for each puppet

skills:
- visual discrimination
- imagination
- storytelling

what you need
- Socks and/or mittens (solid colors work best)
- Embroidery thread and needle
- Permanent marker

what to do
1. Embroider facial features on the foot of the sock or the palm of the mitten or draw them on with markers. (Thread works best on mittens; markers do the job on socks.) If you're using mittens, you can use the thumb as a lower lip, creating a mouth that moves.
2. Tell a story or sing a song using the puppet as the performer.
3. If you've made two mitten puppets, let your child wear them even if they don't match to encourage his early babbling and later storytelling.

The Little Nitty Gritty Band

No doubt, your kitchen contains the makings of a fine band. The range of possibilities for home-made instruments is almost end-less. For infants, just allow access to safe noisemaking materials. For older children, assemble the needed materials and talk about loudness and softness, tempo, and rhythm, demonstrating each

ages: 10 months and up

prep time:
about 5 to 10 minutes for each instrument
skills:
 • listening
 • comparing sounds
 • experimenting

concept. Experiment with your child to see how different ma-terials make different sounds. Create some sound patterns and invite your child to copy them or to compose his own scores.

what you need
• Assorted containers made of different materials, such as metal pots and pans, plastic bowls, tin cans, and cardboard boxes
• Assorted percussion tools made of different materials, such as chopsticks, drinking straws, and wooden, plastic, and metal spoons
• Clean dishtowels

what to do
1. Simply give your child access to the materials and let him first experiment to see what sounds he can make by hitting the percussion tools against the various containers.
2. Demonstrate that different materials and different combi-nations of containers and whackers make different sounds.

3. Fill one or more of the containers with dishtowels to soften the sounds. Cover other containers with the towels to demonstrate another way of softening sounds.
4. Encourage your child to create both loud and soft sounds, vary the tempo, and create sound patterns.

Bathtime Stick-'Ems

Your child will have some good clean fun with these easy-to-make stick-'ems. Begin with the type of plastic placemat that has a slightly spongy feel and that will leave smooth edges when cut.

| **ages:** 10 months and up |
| **prep time:** about 10 minutes |
| **skills:** • eye-hand coordination • imagination |

what you need
• Plastic placemats
• Scissors
• Cookie cutters for patterns (optional)

what to do
1. Trace shapes such as sailboats, people, circles, and squares on the plastic and then cut them out. You may want to use a cookie cutter to make the patterns. For older children, cut the plastic into letter and number shapes.
2. Wet the cutouts and then stick them to the sides of the bathtub or the bathroom wall.
3. Encourage your child to combine various shapes to form pictures. Then invite her to tell a story about her creation.

Shape Sorter

Trying to get the square peg in the round hole is a challenge your toddler is sure to find very amusing—and thought-provoking.

ages: 12 months and up

prep time:
about 10 minutes

skills:
- manual dexterity
- problem solving

what you need
- Shoebox
- A few toy blocks, about 1½"–2" square
- 2 toilet-paper tubes or 1 paper-towel tube
- Pencil
- Scissors
- Craft or utility knife

what to do
1. Use a block and a tube to outline a square and a circle on the top of the shoebox.
2. Using a craft or utility knife, cut out the outlined shapes.
3. Using scissors, cut the tube(s) into six rings, each about 2" wide.
4. Show your child how the blocks and tube rings fit into the matching holes, and let him try his own hand at fitting the shapes.
5. Store the blocks and tube pieces in the shoebox when your child isn't playing with them.

My Costume Corner

A dress-up collection is a must for young children. Keep a supply of cast-off clothing and accessories in a large cardboard box or plastic laundry basket in an accessible place so that when the mood strikes, your child can take on whatever identity suits the moment.

ages: 12 months and up

prep time:
  ongoing
skills:
  • self-dressing
  • imagination

suggested items
• Hats
• Capes
• Grown-up dresses (hemmed or cut short) and/or suit jackets
• Vests
• Handbags and briefcases
• Gloves
• Shoes and boots

what to do
1. Decorate whatever container you've chosen. For instance, cover a cardboard box with festive wrapping paper or self-adhesive vinyl, or tie ribbons on a laundry basket.
2. Place the collection in an accessible place.
3. Provide access to a full-length mirror.
4. Encourage your dressed-up child to tell a story about her new identity. You can even join in the fun!

PARENTS ALERT

Examine all items for loose buttons, stray threads, objects stashed inside of pockets, and any other potential hazards before placing them in the box or basket. Make sure that shoes and boots aren't too large, so that children don't trip while wearing them. Sanitize items by spraying or washing them with disinfectant and airing to dry. Don't place dress-up items or any other toys inside heavy-lidded boxes, which pose a serious hazard.

Sand Table

Sand is a close-to-perfect medium for engaging young children. It's soft and responds easily to little fingers. When wet, sand is easy to form into shapes. It serves as a terrific landscape for little vehicles, and is also great for digging. Because sandboxes are not al-

ages: 12 months and up

prep time:
   about 30 minutes
skills:
   • manual dexterity
   • tactile learning

ways easily accessible and because keeping outdoor boxes sanitary is difficult, a portable indoor sandbox can serve your child's needs well. Begin with an unused cat litter box or clean plastic tub or make your own as follows.

what you need

- Craft or utility knife
- Cardboard box, about 24" square
- Vinyl tablecloth, about 48" square
- Packing or masking tape
- Sand, about 3 lbs.
- Assorted sandbox toys and household items, including small cars and play figures; colanders and funnels for sifting; digging tools, such as spoons and shovels; and beach toys, such as sand molds

what to do

1. If using a ready-made container for your sandbox, skip to Step 3. If making your own sandbox, cut the sides of the box so that it's about 6" deep.
2. Line the box with the vinyl tablecloth, and securely tape the liner in place.
3. Fill the box with sand.
4. Introduce appropriate toys and water to enhance play.
5. To dry the sand between uses, place the box in a sunny window and turn the sand occasionally.

 PARENTS ALERT

Be sure to choose sand that's intended for child play, available through toy stores and art-supply stores.

What's Inside?

This activity is borrowed from the pet store, in the kitty-toy department! And just like a kitten, your toddler can spend lots of time trying to retrieve a toy that's easy to grasp, but challenging to maneuver, through a relatively small space.

ages: 12 months and up
prep time: 15 minutes skills: • visual discrimination • listening • storytelling

what you need
- Craft or utility knife
- Cardboard box, such as a shoebox
- A few hand-size toys, such as a ball, an action figure, and a block
- Tape

what to do
1. Cut two or three holes in the top of the box, just large enough for your toddler's hand to slip through.
2. Place the objects inside the box, and put the lid back on, taping it closed.
3. Shake the box to let your toddler know that something's inside, and invite her to take out the object.

She'll find that it's easy to grasp the object while her hand is inside the box but that, when she makes a fist, it becomes a challenge to remove her hand and the object. You'll see her try various strategies—perhaps lifting and shaking the box to release the objects or holding onto the objects with only her fingertips to pull them through. You might want to suggest strategies or simply sit back and watch her rise to the challenge on her own.

Walk-in Playhouse

A playhouse can set the stage for hours of fun, and give your toddler or preschooler extended experience in pretend play.

ages: 14 months and up
prep time: about an hour
skills: • imagination

what you need
- Large appliance or moving box, about dishwasher size
- Craft or utility knife
- Crayons, markers, paints, or self-adhesive vinyl covering
- Small cardboard boxes, about shoebox size
- Heavy-duty tape
- Fabric
- White glue or paste

what to do
1. Examine the box closely and remove any hazards, such as staples.
2. Draw and then cut away a doorway and windows. If using a tall box such as a refrigerator box, design your playhouse horizontally to avoid toppling.
3. Either cover the entire structure with self-adhesive vinyl or let your child decorate it—inside and out—with paints or crayons.
4. Use small cardboard boxes to add details—a chimney on top, inside storage for play dishes and food, outside window boxes, and so on. Tape them on securely. You can also glue some fabric remnants above the windows for curtains.

All Aboard!

It's a bird! It's a plane! It's . . . well, it's whatever your child wants it to be.

Your child is on the move—climbing, tumbling, and zooming. With this homemade vehicle, she can have hours of adventures.

ages: 18 months and up

prep time: about 1 hour

skills:
• imagination

what you need
- Large, sturdy cardboard box, big enough for your child to sit in
- Packing or masking tape
- Paper fasteners
- Sturdy cardboard sheets (for airplane wings, wheels, steering wheels, and the like)
- Paper-towel tubes (for steering wheels and/or jet engines)
- Scissors and craft or utility knife
- Paper plates (optional)
- 4 jar lids
- Crayons

what to do
1. Examine the box closely and remove any hazards, such as staples.
2. Use the scissors or knife as appropriate to cut off the top flaps from the box. Save the flaps to use for airplane wings or other vehicle parts.
3. Reinforce the outer seams of the box with packing or masking tape.
4. Help your child decide what kind of vehicle she would like

to make. (See below for adding wings, car wheels, and steering wheels.)

5. Let your child decorate her vehicle with crayons.

Airplane

1. Cut wing shapes from cardboard. Cut horizontal slits toward the center of the longer sides of the box, and insert the cardboard "wings."
2. Tape the wings in place with packing or masking tape both inside and outside of the box.
3. Tape a paper-towel tube below each wing to make "jet engines."

Car wheel

1. Use the point of the scissors or the knife to make a hole near the bottom corner of each long side of the box for attaching "wheels."
2. For wheels, use paper plates or cut out 8"-diameter cardboard rounds. Attach the wheels with paper fasteners, head-side out.
3. To ensure that the ends of the paper fasteners inside the box don't scratch your child as she sits inside the "car," encase the ends of the fasteners under jar lids, holding the lids in place with packing or masking tape.

Steering wheel

1. Cut a round hole the size of a paper-towel tube into the front of the vehicle, where the "steering column" will be placed.
2. For the "steering wheel," use a sturdy paper plate or cut a cardboard circle, about 8" in diameter. Cut a circle, the same size as the paper-towel tube, into the center of the steering wheel and securely tape the circle to one end of the tube.
3. Slide the other end of the tube into the hole in the box. Your child can turn the tube wheel stem to "steer" the vehicle.

Felt Art Board

Here's some no-fuss, no-muss art-work for your child—and a plea-sure for you, too.

ages: 20 months and up
prep time: about 30 minutes
skills: • eye-hand coordination • imagination

what you need

- Heavy cardboard, about 2' × 3'
- Neutral-color felt, about 2½' × 3½'
- Heavy-duty tape
- Felt scraps, assorted colors
- Scissors
- Cookie cutters for patterns (optional)

what to do

1. Stretch the piece of neutral felt over the cardboard, securing the excess felt on the back of the board with heavy-duty tape.
2. Cut out various shapes from the colorful felt scraps. Include geometric shapes and shapes representative of familiar objects, such as animals, vehicles, or pieces of fruit. Use cookie cutters for patterns if you wish.
3. Demonstrate how the felt cutouts adhere to the board and are easily removed and repositioned.
4. Give your child plenty of time to create his own master-piece.

Dinner Party

While store-bought toy food and
a child-size table-and-chair set
lend authenticity to a make-
believe dinner party, you don't
need to invest in these items to
have an enjoyable at-home feast.
A sturdy box, turned upside
down, can make a fine toddler-
size table. Paper plates and cups
are a safe and inexpensive sub-
stitute for toy dishes. (Or you can use your child's own plastic
tableware.) Dinner guests can include any or all of your
child's stuffed animals, dolls, or action figures—and, of
course, you.

ages: 20 months and up
prep time: about 10 minutes
skills: • imagination • social skills • math skills

what you need
- Small table or overturned box
- Tableware
- Vase of flowers (optional)
- Real or imaginary food
- Construction paper
- Crayons or markers

what to do
1. Invite your child to help set the table, encouraging him to set one place for each guest.
2. If you wish, add some atmosphere by placing a flower in a vase on the table.
3. Help your child make a menu out of construction paper for guests to read. Illustrate the menu with cutout pictures.

4. Serve real or imaginary food.
5. Take turns being the server and the guest with your child.

---

extra!

Cut out pictures of food for serving. Ads and food pages of magazines are terrific sources of right-size photos. Your child can help you scan magazines for appropriate pictures.

---

the menu

If your guest list includes real people, serve up some food that your toddler can help prepare

Some suggestions:

- Sliced bananas served with a yogurt dip
- Cheese sandwiches cut into cookie-cutter shapes
- Soft pretzels
- Apple juice served in teacups

A Dozen Things to Do with a Cardboard Tube

Three cheers to whomever invented the humble paper-towel and toilet-paper tubes! These cardboard cylinders serve myriad purposes, many particularly delightful to young children. Here are a dozen ways to recycle tubes and have fun with your toddler:

> **ages:** 24 months and up
>
> **prep time:**
>   none more than 1 minute
> **skills:**
>   • eye-hand coordination
>   • imagination
>   • listening
>   • experimenting

1 **Phone.** Hold a tube to your child's ear and talk softly. Then encourage him to talk to you through the tube.

2 **Chute.** Demonstrate dropping objects through the tube. Choose items too large (such as a toy car) to pose a choking hazard.

3 **Musical instrument.** Bang two tubes together. Use one as a drumstick. Hum into one to hear and feel the vibration.

4 **"Popper."** Place a rolled-up thank-you note for coming to a party inside, wrap the tube in tissue or wrapping paper, and tie each end with a ribbon. These "poppers," a traditional Victorian party favor, make pretty party table decorations, too.

5 **Rings.** Slice a paper-towel tube into 2" rings. Encourage your child to string the rings onto any holder, such as a

ruler or a piece of yarn. Or make a tabletop ring-toss game by placing a small, heavy object, such as a salt shaker, on the table and encouraging your child to drop the rings over it.

6 **Shape cutter.** After your child pats down some clay, show her how to make circles by pressing one end of the tube into the slab.

7 **Paintbrush.** Dip one end of the tube into a small amount of poster paint and transfer the circle design onto a piece of paper. Help your child make faces, flowers, or other circular designs.

8 **Racing rollers.** Create a ramp from a board or large piece of cardboard. Show your child how to place the tube at the top and watch it roll down. For added fun, have a tube race, using two or more tubes.

9 **Doll and teddy cast.** When children experience or observe a playmate wearing a cast on an arm or leg, the game of placing a "cast" on a favored toy is particularly appealing. Simply slip the tube over the "injured" limb.

10 **Crayon case.** Cover one end of the tube with tape. Use a 4" square of paper secured with a rubber band for a lid on the other end. The tube makes a great carrying case for crayons.

11 **Art-storage tube.** To save your child's artwork, roll his drawing and place it inside the paper-towel tube. To use the tube as a mailer—so you can share the artwork with relatives—simply tape the ends closed, and place a mailing label on the outside.

12 **Telescope.** Give your child a paper-towel tube to look through and pretend that it's a telescope. Or tape two toilet-paper tubes together to make pretend binoculars.

Lead an expedition through the backyard or your local park, hunting down "wild animals" such as squirrels, birds, ants, and whatever else you're likely to see.

★ Also see "Shape Sorter" on page 11 and "Rocket" on page 41.

Little People Theater

Any doorway can make a grand theater. And this puppet theater is easily stored when not in use. Your child can use this theater as a stage for her stuffed animals and action figures, as well as for puppets or even for her own performance.

ages: 24 months and up

prep time:
  about 5 minutes
skills:
  • imagination
  • storytelling

what you need
• 1 pair of café curtains
• Clip-on curtain rings
• 1 tension curtain rod, sized for a conveniently located doorway

what to do
1. Make, purchase, or recycle brightly colored café curtains, and clip the rings onto them. Place the curtains on the tension rod.
2. Place the rod in a doorway.

3. Show your child how to have her puppets perform above the stage curtain.
4. Gather an appreciative audience, and let the show begin.

---

extra!

Use a second tension curtain rod and pair of curtains to make the theater more authentic. Just place the second rod above the first and show your child how to slide the upper curtains open or closed to begin and end each show.

Picture Match

With a deck of about 10 to 20 cards, your child can play a number of mixing and matching games.

ages: 24 months and up

prep time: about 30 minutes

skills:
- categorizing
- matching

what you need
- Scissors
- Magazine pictures
- White glue, glue stick, paste, or double-sided tape
- Index cards

what to do
1. Collect and cut out a number of magazine pictures that can be grouped in a variety of ways. For instance, cut out two pictures each of dogs, babies, foods, houses, and cars.

2. Glue or tape each picture onto a separate card.
3. Ask your child to find pairs of like objects.
4. Vary this game by categorizing by different attributes: Have your child find all the cards that contain pictures of round things, red things, or things with eyes, for example.

Cookie-Cutter Creations

Cookie cutters are great for more than cookie-making. Put an extra set in your child's art-supply box for hours of fun. Consider these possibilities:

ages: 24 months and up

prep time:
under 1 minute

skills:
- eye-hand coordination
- creativity

Traced patterns. Demonstrate using a crayon to trace the cookie-cutter shapes onto paper.

Sand sculptures. Use the cutters to make imprints in wet sand.

Clay cutouts. Roll out clay or play clay about ½" thick, press with the cutter, and lift away the excess, just as you would to make cookies. Gently pry the material free. (Covering the cookie cutter with a light dusting of flour will help keep the clay or play clay from sticking.)

Cookie-cutter wind chimes. Their light weight and interesting shapes make metal cookie cutters great components for a wind chime. Just string equal lengths of thin ribbon or string through each cutter and attach them to a wire hanger, tying the strings about 2" apart.

Stamps. Pour some finger-paint on a paper plate. Carefully dip in a cookie cutter, and then press it onto paper to transfer the design.

It's always fun to make real cookies, too!

Six New Uses for Aluminum Foil

Aluminum foil is a great medium for lots of different projects:

ages: 24 months and up	
prep time: varies **skills:** • manual dexterity • eye-hand coordination • creativity	

1 **Drawing board.** Place a layer of foil over a magazine and let your child make designs on it with a dull-pointed pencil, dried-out ballpoint pen, or blunt-ended chopstick.

2 **Sculpture.** A ball of foil can be shaped easily into a variety of shapes. Demonstrate making a few and let your child create his own.

3 **Molds.** Press the foil over any rigid object, such as a bowl or action figure, and let your child use the mold to make mud or wet-sand creations. For smaller objects, regular-weight foil works well. For larger objects, use heavy-duty foil.

4 **Bowl and balls.** Mold one piece of foil into a bowl shape and other pieces into balls. Show your child how to toss the balls into the bowl.

5 **Hoops.** Roll a piece of foil into a snake shape and curl it into a hoop. Make a large foil ball and flatten one end. Then put a pencil or other dowel into this mound. Show your child how to toss the ring onto the pole.

6 **Life mask.** Gently mold heavy-duty foil over your child's face, outlining each of his features. Carefully remove the molding and you—and he—have a perfect foil replica of your child. If he expresses discomfort, stop making the mask and remove the aluminum foil. Do not allow your child to place aluminum foil over his face unsupervised.

Paper-Bag Dress-Up

The lowly paper grocery bag is a costume collection in disguise. For all of the following, the bag will be worn bottom-up.

ages: 30 months and up

prep time:
varies, averaging 10 minutes
skills:
• imagination

what you need
• Scissors
• Grocery-size brown paper bags
• Masking tape
• Crayons
• Aluminum foil, ribbons, and other decorative accessories (optional)

what to do

To make a Western vest

1. Create the vest-front opening through the middle of one wide side of the bag by cutting straight down from the top open edge to about 2" into the bottom of the bag. Be sure to cut through only one layer.
2. At the end of the slit on the bottom of the bag, cut a circle large enough to be the neck hole for your child.
3. Cut out an armhole on each narrow side of the bag near the bottom.
4. To reinforce the bag and make the vest more comfortable, cover all the cut edges with masking tape.
5. To make fringes along the bottom of the vest, cut 2"-deep slits along the top edge of the bag, spacing the slits about 1" apart.
6. Let your child decorate the vest by drawing on a sheriff's badge or other ornamental designs.

To make a hula skirt

1. Create the waistline by cutting from the top open edge straight to the center of the bag bottom. Then cut out a circle the size of your child's waist from the bottom of the bag.
2. To reinforce the bag and make the skirt more comfortable, cover the waistline with masking tape.
3. To make the grass fringe, cut additional slits perpendicular to the top edge of the bag (the "hemline"), spacing them about 1" apart and stopping each about 3" from the waistline. If you miscut the fringe where the bag folds near the waistline, just tape the pieces back together.

To make a robot suit

1. Cut a circle in the bottom of the bag, large enough for your child's head to fit through. If the bag is too narrow for your child to pull down over his body without tearing it, cut a slit in one of the long, wide sides of the bag.
2. Cut out an armhole on each narrow side of the bag near the bottom.

3. To reinforce the bag and make the suit more comfortable, cover all the cut edges with masking tape.
4. Cut the sleeves from a second bag. First, cut away the bottom of the bag. From the remaining portion, cut two 10"-wide strips the length of your child's arms. Roll each strip into a tube and tape the seam closed. (Depending upon your child's age, he may be uncomfortable wearing the sleeves; if so, omit this step.)
5. Cover each piece with aluminum foil or have your child color all the pieces with silver crayon.
6. Have your child put on the body of the suit before attaching the sleeves. If you cut a slit in the bag, the slit should be in the back.
7. Slide on the sleeves and tape them to the body of the suit. Tape the back slit closed.

Surprise Picture Book

Here's a mystery book for the very youngest detectives.

what you need
- Variety of 8½" × 11" pictures cut from magazines
- Spiral notebook, about 8½" × 11"
- Tape
- Scissors

ages: 3 years and up

prep time:
  about 10 minutes
skills:
- visual discrimination
- problem solving

what to do

1. Tape the pictures to every other right-hand page of the spiral notebook, skipping the first page.
2. Cut horizontal strips—two to five per page—almost all the way to the spiral binding on the pages of the notebook on which there are no pictures.
3. Have your child turn one strip at a time, revealing a portion of the picture underneath.
4. Encourage her to guess the picture before it's completely uncovered.

Go Fishing

There's nothing like a lazy day of fishing to help your child catch some fun.

ages: 3 years and up	
prep time: about 10 minutes **skills:**	
• manual dexterity • eye-hand coordination	

what you need

- Smooth stick, about 12" long
- String, about 18" long
- Small magnet
- Pencil
- Construction paper, assorted colors
- Scissors
- Paper clips
- Cardboard box, plastic bucket, wading pool, or other container

what to do

1. Tie the string securely to one end of the stick.
2. Tie the magnet to the other end of the string.

3. Draw fish shapes on the construction paper and cut them out.
4. Fasten a paper clip to the nose of each fish.
5. Place the fish in a "pond," such as a big box or empty wading pool. Show your child how to fish using your homemade rod. The magnet will attract the fish. Take turns pulling in the line.

---

extra!

Add some authenticity to your child's fishing experience by making the fish out of craft foam or plastic placemats and floating them in a wading-pool "pond."

 PARENTS ALERT

Always closely supervise children when playing with water. Even small amounts can pose a danger to children under the age of 3.

Bubble Wands

There's no limit to the number, size, and shape in which you can create bubbles.

ages: 3 years and up
prep time: 20 minutes
skills:
• manual dexterity
• understanding the properties of bubbles

what you need
- Pipe cleaners for smaller wands
- Wire for larger wands (cut from clothing hangers or other source)
- Commercial or homemade bubble mix (see page 5)

what to do
1. For smaller wands, twist pipe cleaners into interesting shapes, such as stars and hearts, leaving a handle of about 3". For larger wands, twist the wire into circle and oval shapes, leaving about a 6" handle.
2. Pour bubble mix to a depth of 1" to 2" in a container as wide as the wand shape you're making.
3. Simply dip the wand into the bubble mix and let the fun begin.

★   Also see "Inside a Giant Bubble" on page 56.

Rainbow Crayons

Here's a great way for your child
to transform that abundance of
broken crayons into the most de-
sirable crayons in his or her collection.

what you need
- Broken crayons
- Disposable cupcake tin
- Nonstick cooking spray

ages: 3 years and up

prep time:
  20 minutes
skills:
  • understanding
    colors and the
    processes of
    melting with heat
    and hardening with
    coolness

what to do
1. Heat the oven to 300°F.
2. Remove the paper wrapping from the crayons and break
   the crayons into 1" or smaller pieces.
3. Spray nonstick cooking spray into each cup of the cupcake
   tin.
4. Fill each cup half full with crayon pieces of different colors.
5. Place the filled tin in the oven and bake for about 6 minutes
   or until all the crayons have partially melted. Be sure not
   to let them melt thoroughly or the wax will blend into one
   grayish color. They may also begin to smell if they get too
   hot.
6. Let cool and then remove the wax cakes from the cupcake
   tins to have new, fist-sized, speckled-color crayons.

★ Also see "Stained-Glass Windows with Crayons" on page
   61 for another way to reuse old crayons.

---

extra!

For a slightly different effect, melt one color at a time in the cupcake tin. Let that color harden and then add the next color on top and melt again. Let each color cool and harden before adding the next color. This process will create rainbow-striped crayons.

Batik Art

Whether kids create a wall hanging or a wearable work of art—such as a T-shirt—batik and kids go together.

ages: 3 years and up

prep time:
30 minutes

skills:
- creativity

what you need
- Plain piece of cloth, such as a napkin or T-shirt
- Crayons
- 2 damp paper towels
- Iron

what to do
1. Have your child draw—leaning heavily on the crayon—on a piece of cloth. He can use one or many different colors. The waxy color should be thickly applied.
2. Place the damp paper towels over the design.

3. Iron the paper towels until they are dry. The wax will melt and set into the fabric. If using a T-shirt, place a piece of cardboard inside to keep the wax from bleeding onto the back.

I'm a Puppet!

Your child will enjoy taking center stage as she directs herself in this play.

ages: 3 years and up
prep time: about 10 minutes
skills: • imagination • storytelling

what you need
- Photos of your child's favorite people—herself, her family, and even her pets
- Scissors
- Craft sticks
- Double-sided tape, white glue, or paste
- Magazine pictures, cardboard, and clear self-adhesive vinyl covering (optional)

what to do
1. Cut out the photos to create silhouettes.
2. Tape or glue each figure onto a craft stick.
3. Encourage your child to tell stories about the characters' adventures. She may even want to perform the story on her own homemade TV. (See page 88.)

extra!

As an alternative to photos, look through magazines and catalogs for characters that have special appeal to your child, such as Elmo or Blue, the canine star of *Blue's Clues*. Cover these pictures with clear self-adhesive vinyl and attach them to cardboard so that they'll be sturdy enough to do their "stand-up" acts. Or make stick figures of your child's favorite storybook characters and have them perform as you read.

Sewing Cards

Here are two easy ways to create sewing cards that can keep your preschooler busy for long stretches at a time.

ages: 3 years and up

prep time:
  about 10 minutes per card

skills:
  • manual dexterity
  • eye-hand coordination

what you need
• Sturdy pieces of cardboard, each about 6" × 6"
• Scissors or one-hole punch
• Yarn or shoelaces with nubs

what to do
For younger children
1. Cut three or four V-shaped notches on each side of the cardboard square.

2. Cut the yarn to about a 20" length.
3. Demonstrate crisscrossing the square with the yarn to create various patterns.

For older kids

1. Use a one-hole punch to make 10 to 15 holes in the cardboard square—either randomly or to outline a particular shape.
2. Provide a shoelace, about 24" long. Choose one with a stiff nub to make sewing easier.
3. Demonstrate threading the shoelace in and out of the holes.

Your child can reuse the cards, or you can tape the ends of the yarn or shoelace to the back of the cardboard and display her handiwork.

 PARENTS ALERT

Always closely supervise children under age 4 when playing with lengths of string or ribbon to prevent strangulation.

Mailbox

Getting mail is a special experience for a youngster, and this activity allows your child to receive and send mail every day.

ages: 3 years and up
prep time: 20 minutes
skills: • manual dexterity • written communication

what you need
- Box, big enough to be a mailbox (from shoebox to carton size)
- Markers and paints
- Paper and envelopes
- Scissors
- Pencils
- Stamps, such as those that accompany sweepstakes mailings (optional)
- White glue or paste

what to do
1. Decorate the box with markers and paint.
2. Make some special stamps by cutting paper into small pieces and drawing pictures on them, or use stamps from sweepstakes mailings.
3. Write your child a letter, put it in an envelope, stamp it, and "mail" it in the box.
4. Encourage your child to write back, using drawings or your transcriptions of dictation, and mail the letter in the box for you or other family members to receive.

Trace Me

This is a favorite kindergarten activity that you can do at home. It makes a terrific bedroom or closet-door decoration. It's also fun to do at six-month or yearly intervals so your child can observe his growth over time.

ages: 3 years and up

prep time:
  30 minutes
skills:
  • learning about self
  • creativity

what you need
- Piece of paper as tall as your child (piece together brown grocery bags or newspapers, if a single sheet is not available)
- Markers and crayons
- Scissors

what to do
1. Have your child lie down on the paper, and trace his outline.
2. Have your child color in his face and an outfit on the outline.
3. Cut out the form.

Rocket

Create a rocket ship and blast off!

what you need

- Scissors
- Paper-towel tube
- Aluminum foil or paints, crayons, and markers
- Piece of cardboard, at least 6" square
- Construction paper
- Tape

ages: 3 years and up
prep time: 15 minutes skills: • manual dexterity • counting backwards

what to do

1. Cut three 2"-long slits at equal intervals at one end of a paper-towel tube.
2. Allow your child to decorate the tube either by covering it with foil or by coloring or painting it.
3. Cut three corner triangles from a piece of cardboard, with the sides of each corner measuring at least 2". Again, add decoration by covering or coloring each triangle.
4. Insert the triangles into the slits on the paper-towel tube to allow the "rocket" to stand upright. Tape the triangles in place.
5. Cut a pie shape from construction paper. Bend it to form a cone. Tape the cone closed and then tape it from the inside onto the other end of the rocket.
6. Countdown—10 . . . 9 . . . 8 . . . 7 . . . 6 . . . 5 . . . 4 . . . 3 . . . 2 . . . 1! Now blast off!

---

extra!

Other ways to enjoy this rocket include:

- Turn it into a mobile. Tape a length of string or fishing line about 5" from the base and attach the other end of the string or line to a ceiling fixture.

- Create a rocket party-loot holders. Make enough rockets for party guests and fill each one with treats. Cut a notch in the bottom edge of each triangle close to the rocket base, so you'll be able to cover the open end with a piece of wax paper secured with a rubber band. Place treats in the tube before covering the end.

Star in a TV Show

If your child loves TV but needs encouragement toward more active play, let him star in his own production in this homemade box.

what you need
- Cardboard box, large enough for your child to stand in, or a piece of poster board or cardboard, about 24" × 36"
- Ruler

| **ages:** 3 years and up |
| **prep time:** 30 minutes |
| **skills:** |
| • making up stories |
| • retelling stories |
| • putting events in sequence |

- Pencil
- Utility knife
- Crayons or markers
- Stuffed animals, puppets, or other props

what to do

1. If you're using a box, inspect it carefully and remove hazards such as staples.
2. Measure and trace an opening about 12" × 16" on the front of the box, poster board, or cardboard, and cut it out to create a TV screen.
3. Have your child decorate the outside of the box or the piece of poster board or cardboard to resemble a TV.
4. Encourage your child to stand behind the screen and act out scenes from his favorite show. If he has stuffed animals or dolls of the show characters, let him work them into the script, too.

Monster Mouth

What do you feed a hungry monster? Anything it wants! With this creation, your child and some friends can have loads of fun as they practice their throwing skills.

what you need

- Large cardboard box
- Markers or crayons
- Craft or utility knife

ages: 4 years and up
prep time: 10 minutes
skills:
• manual dexterity
• imagination
• eye-hand coordination

what to do

1. Have your child design a large picture of an open mouth on the side of the box. It can be scary with big teeth or friendly with a big lipsticky smile.
2. Cut away the opening in the mouth.
3. Let your child toss balls, crumbled paper, or even Frisbees inside. See how much the monster can eat.

Big-Kid Musical Instruments

This project provides an inexpensive introduction to real musical instruments. Read the directions through to see which materials you'll need for the different instruments.

ages: 4 years and up
prep time: 15 minutes or less per instrument
skills:
• manual dexterity
• understanding sound

what you need

- Any clean, nonbreakable items that can be used for making sounds, such as wooden blocks and dowels, cardboard boxes, tin cans with smoothed edges, plastic bottles in different sizes, plastic drinking straws, metal pipes, and cardboard tubing
- Pictures of real musical instruments
- Tape
- Rubber bands

what to do

1. Review pictures of musical instruments with your child. Discuss their attributes, noting that some have strings to pluck or strum, some are hollow, and some are played by blowing or by hitting.
2. Choose an instruments to make and gather the materials.
3. Strike up the band!

Soda-bottle pipe organ. Line up four to six empty plastic soda bottles of different sizes and tape them together in a row, from shortest to tallest. Blow across the top of each bottle. Notice that each bottle produces a different sound. (Larger bottles have a lower pitch, and smaller ones have a higher pitch.)

Drinking-straw mouth pipe. Cut five plastic drinking straws into different lengths—from about 3" to 8". Flatten one end of each straw, and cut on an angle to form a point. Lay out the straws in size order, aligning the pointy ends, and tape them together. Blow directly into the pointy end of each "pipe," noticing the differences in sound. (As the straw size increases, the pitch becomes lower.)

Shoebox guitar. Using four or more rubber bands in a range of thicknesses and an open, uncovered shoebox, place the rubber bands, in order of their thickness, around the box lengthwise, and encourage your child to pluck and strum the strings. How does the sound of each string differ? (Thinner strings have a higher pitch, and thicker ones have a lower pitch.)

★ For ideas for making musical instruments for younger children, see "Maracas" on page 7.

Personalized Puzzles

Because kids are always losing pieces to puzzles, keeping them on hand can prove to be a real challenge. Here is a great—and very personal—way to replenish your puzzle collection.

ages: 4 years and up
prep time: 20 minutes
skills: • eye-hand coordination • critical thinking • understanding shapes

what you need
- Piece of cardboard, at least 4" × 6"
- Photograph, same size as the cardboard; or markers, crayons, or paints
- White glue or paste (if using a photograph)
- Clear self-adhesive vinyl covering
- Scissors

what to do
1. Glue the photo onto the cardboard, or draw or paint a picture directly on the cardboard.
2. For added fun, have your child create an additional drawing on the back side of the cardboard—he'll have a two-sided puzzle.
3. Cover the photo or drawing with clear self-adhesive vinyl, and smooth out any bubbles.
4. Cut the picture into jigsaw-type shapes, making bigger pieces for young children and smaller pieces for older ones.

---

extra!

Older kids will also enjoy creating written-message jigsaw puzzles to pass along to friends.

Puffy Paintings

Adding dimension to his artwork will surely excite your child. With your instructions and supervision, your child can make puffy paintings by himself.

ages: 4 years and up

prep time:
  20 minutes
skills:
  • imagination
  • eye-hand
    coordination
  • artistic expression

what you need
- Plain white paper, 2 or more sheets
- Markers or crayons
- Scissors
- Pencil
- White glue or paste
- Plastic drinking straw

what to do
1. Have your child draw a picture, such as a flower or a fish, on one sheet of paper. The drawing should be no larger than 4" × 8".
2. Cut out the drawing.
3. Trace the outline onto the second sheet of paper and cut it out.
4. Carefully glue the two sheets together along the edges, leaving a ½" opening on one edge. Let the glue dry thoroughly.
5. Insert the straw into the opening and blow gently, filling the pocket between the two cutouts with air.
6. When the art is puffed full of air, either remove the straw and glue the opening closed, or if the straw can be incorporated into the art—such as serving as the flower stem—glue it in position, blow more air into it, and tape the open end closed.

Pushpin Art

Kids will "light up" with this easy
trick. Younger kids can draw a
design on paper for you to use as
your pin-art guide. Kids over 6 or
so can do the pushpinning, too,
with your supervision.

ages: 4 years and up

prep time:
  5 minutes
skills:
  • manual dexterity
  • creativity
  • understanding light

What you need
• Newspaper
• Plain white paper
• Masking tape
• Pencil
• Pushpin

What to do
1. Layer the newspaper to make sure that it's thick enough to
   prevent a pushed-in pushpin from penetrating all the way
   through.
2. Tape a plain sheet of paper to the top of the newspaper pile.
3. With the pencil, draw an outline of the design you want to
   create on the paper. Keep it simple.
4. Using a pushpin, create your pushpin art by piercing the
   paper along the drawn outline. Make sure the holes are
   close enough together to form a recognizable design, but
   not so close as to tear the paper.
5. When the perforated design is completed, remove the
   masking tape.
6. Tape the picture to a window and watch the light shine
   through. Or, in a dark room, illuminate the design by holding it in front of a flashlight.

Butterfly Wings

Before beginning this activity, review real or pictured butterflies
with your child, noting the beautiful wing markings and the fact
that the wings are symmetrical—
identical but reversed on both
sides of the body.

ages: 4 years and up
prep time:
5 minutes
skills:
• manual dexterity
• understanding
symmetry

what you need
- Plain white paper
- Finger-paints
- Pencil
- Scissors

what to do
1. Fold the paper in half, and then unfold it and place it like an open book on the table.
2. Let your child dab a few drops of paint of various colors onto the paper, working on one side of the crease only.
3. While the paint is wet, refold the paper and gently press the two halves together.
4. On the outside of the folded paper, draw the shape of a butterfly wing, so that the "body" of the butterfly is against the fold.
5. Cut through the two layers of paper along the shape of the butterfly.
6. Open the paper and let your child enjoy the unique butterfly-wing pattern he's created.

Magic Message Board

This activity not only lets your child create a message board, but gives her the chance to watch a crayon disappear!

ages: 4 years and up
prep time: 10 minutes **skills:** • creativity • understanding the qualities of wax crayons and wax paper

what you need
- Cardboard
- Old crayons, with paper wrapping removed
- Wax paper, cut to the width of the cardboard, and about 2" longer than the length of the cardboard
- Tape
- Stylus, such as an empty ballpoint pen or a chopstick

what to do
1. Have your child completely cover the cardboard with a crayoned layer of color (one color or many). This process usually works best using the sides rather than the points of crayons. The crayons will wear down nearly completely.
2. Lay the wax paper over the colored board, folding the 2" excess over the top and taping it in place.
3. Let your child make a simple line drawing or write a message on the wax paper, pressing hard with the stylus. The wax paper will stick to the waxy crayon covering to reveal the drawing or message.
4. Pull up the wax paper to erase the drawing or message and start again. Replace the wax paper if it becomes torn.

What's in the Tent?

This is perfect for a rainy day.

ages: 4 years and up
prep time: 15 minutes
skills:
• creativity
• understanding light and shadow

what you need
- Large white or light-colored bedsheet
- Chairs or other support structures to form the frame of a tent
- Flashlight

what to do
1. Drape the sheet over the backs of two or more chairs, leaving enough room for a person to crawl into this "tent."
2. Turn off the room lights.
3. Take turns with your child going inside the tent with a flashlight. Place the flashlight on the seat of the chair, aiming the beam of light in front of the person inside the tent.
4. Whoever is inside the tent should act out the behavior of an animal or other creature; the person outside must guess what the other is pretending to be.

Sponge Stamps

Instead of expensive store-bought rubber stamps, try these easy-to-make alternatives.

ages: 4 years and up
prep time: 15 minutes
skills: • manual dexterity • creativity

what you need
- Clean sponges
- Marker
- Scissors
- Finger-paints and paper plates, or ink pads
- Plain white paper

what to do
1. Have your child outline shapes, such as stars or letters, on one or more sponges with the marker.
2. Cut along the drawn outline with scissors. (Cutting is often easier with a slightly damp sponge. If you dampen the sponge before cutting, let it dry before applying paint or ink.)
3. Pour a little finger-paint on a paper plate, using a separate plate for each color; or provide your child with colored ink pads.
4. Lightly dip the sponge cutout into the paint or press the sponge gently into an ink pad, being sure to cover the entire shape with paint or ink.
5. Transfer the design onto plain paper.

extra!

Here are a few more ways to use sponge stamps:

- Create stamps for each letter of your child's name and let her make a sign for her door or personalize a favorite wooden chair.

- Apply the design to a roll of brown paper to make unique gift wrap.

- Decorate a clay flowerpot or wooden window box with sponge-stamp designs.

Mixed-Media Art

There's no need to stick to one form of artistic expression on a single piece of paper. Let your child mix crayons and watercolor paints for some truly amazing results.

ages: 4 years and up

prep time:
 5 minutes
skills:
- creativity
- understanding the qualities of wax crayons and watercolor paints

what you need
- Paper
- Crayons
- Watercolor paints
- Paintbrush

what to do

1. Have your child draw a design on a sheet of paper with the crayons.
2. Use watercolors to paint over the design. The paint will not adhere to the crayon section but instead will spread all around it, creating a vibrant burst of color.
3. To maintain the burst effect, keep the paper flat while it dries. Or, to create a different look, tilt the paper while the watercolors are still wet.

Bouncing Clown

Bring the circus home with this high-flying act.

ages: 4 years and up
prep time: 15 minutes skills: • understanding balance

what you need

- Coat hanger (wire dry-cleaner variety)
- Wire cutters
- Corks or heavy-duty tape
- Paper
- Markers
- Scissors
- Tape

what to do

1. Cut a 20" length of coat hanger, and bend it to form a heart shape, with the ends close to one another but not touching. Discard the leftover top of the hanger.
2. Place a cork on each end of the cut wire or cover the points with heavy-duty tape to prevent scratches on people or furniture.

3. Draw and cut out a picture of a silly clown, about 8" tall and 6" wide, with arms and legs extended.
4. Tape the extended arms to the inside of the heart-shaped hanger.
5. Hang one end of the heart shape onto the edge of a table.
6. Give it a slight nudge and watch the clown bounce and dance.

Copy Machine

Though it's decidedly low-tech, this means of making copies encourages careful attention to detail.

ages: 4 years and up

prep time:
  15 minutes
skills:
  • creativity
  • making impressions

what you need
• Plain white paper, 2 sheets
• Crayon
• Pencil

what to do
1. Have your child completely cover one sheet of paper with crayon, building up a waxy base.
2. Place the crayoned paper, face down, over the other sheet of paper.
3. Using a pencil, have your child draw a picture, leaning somewhat heavily, on the top sheet (the back of the crayoned sheet). The drawing created on the top will be reproduced on the bottom sheet.

Inside a Giant Bubble

This giant bubble makes a terrific outdoor summer party activity.

ages: 4 years and up

prep time:
  20 minutes
skills:
  • manual dexterity
  • experimenting

what you need

- Hula hoop, about 18" diameter; or rope, about 1" thick and 48" long
- Heavy-duty tape
- 1–1½ cups commercial or homemade bubble mix (see page 5)
- Wading pool or plastic basin, at least 36" diameter

what to do

1. If not using a hula hoop, form the rope into a circle and tape the ends together securely.
2. Pour the bubble mix into the wading pool or basin, and add water, filling the container about 3" deep.
3. Place the hoop or circle of rope in the center of the pool or basin.
4. Dress your child in her bathing suit and have her stand in the middle of the hoop or rope. (Have her wear goggles if she's afraid of getting soap in her eyes.)
5. Gently lift up the hoop or rope, encasing your child in a huge bubble. Let her blow or poke her way out.

PARENTS ALERT

Always closely supervise children when playing with water. Even small amounts can pose a danger to children under the age of 3.

Tissue-Mosaic Flowerpots and Vases

When your child is wondering what to make for a great gift (one for you, perhaps?), this suggestion is bound to be met with enthusiasm.

ages: 4 years and up

prep time:
  20 minutes, on two
  separate days
skills:
  • manual dexterity
  • design concepts

what you need
• Tissue paper, assorted colors
• Scissors
• White glue or paste
• Paper plate
• Glass soda or milk bottle or small clay flowerpot
• 2 paintbrushes, 1"–1½" wide

what to do

1. Cut or tear the tissue paper into a variety of small shapes.
2. Pour some glue onto a paper plate and dip one of the paint-brushes into it. Paint the glue onto the bottle or pot.
3. Gently lay the tissue-paper shapes onto the gluey surface.
4. Continue layering until the pot or bottle is completely covered with tissue paper.
5. Let the glue dry overnight.
6. With the second paintbrush, paint the entire surface of the pot or bottle with another layer of glue to seal the tissue paper. Let dry.

Life-Size Scarecrow

This character is just right for welcoming guests during the Halloween season.

what you need

- Outgrown clothing, including shirts, pants, shoes, socks, and a hat
- Newspaper, crumpled; or straw
- Belt or rope
- Balloon or beach ball and a face mask, or a plastic jack-o'-lantern
- Tape or string
- Outdoor chair
- Crate or other footrest (optional)

ages: 4 years and up

prep time:
about an hour
skills:
- creativity
- imagination
- dressing skills

what to do

1. Stuff the shirt, pants, and socks with newspaper or straw, until the clothing takes on form.
2. Place the stuffed shirt and pants on the chair in a sitting position. Secure them to the chair with a belt or rope, if necessary.
3. Tape or tie the balloon, beach ball, or plastic jack-o'-lantern to the neck opening. If you use a balloon or beach ball, cover it with a face mask.
4. Put a hat over the head, securing it with tape, if necessary.
5. Put the socks into the shoes and position them under the stuffed pants legs. (If the legs are too short to reach the floor, prop the feet on a crate or other footrest.)

Motorized Car

This little "car" operates on its own power.

what you need

- Paper clip
- Rubber band
- Empty thread spool
- Metal washer
- Cotton swab

ages: 4 years and up	
prep time: 15 minutes	
skills:	
• manual dexterity	
• basic physics	

what to do

1. Slip the paper clip onto the rubber band, so that it dangles.
2. Thread the rubber band through the hole in the spool, with the clip remaining at the other end of the spool.

3. Thread the extending rubber-band loop through the metal washer, and then insert the cotton swab in the rubber-band loop.
4. Twirl the cotton swab as tightly as possible.
5. Put the spool down on its side and watch it skip across the floor.

Stained-Glass Windows with Paper

This pretty window decoration gives you and your child a meaningful way to talk about shape, color, and design.

ages: 4 years and up

prep time:
  20 minutes
skills:
  • manual dexterity
  • design concepts

what you need
• Tissue paper, assorted colors
• Scissors
• Liquid starch (available at any supermarket)
• Paper plate
• 2 sheets of wax paper, each about 9" × 12"
• Paintbrush, 1" — 1½" wide
• Iron and ironing board
• Paper towels

what to do
1. Have your child cut or tear the tissue paper into a variety of shapes.
2. Pour some liquid starch onto the paper plate and dip the paintbrush into it. Paint the first sheet of wax paper with the starch.

3. Have your child gently lay the tissue-paper cutouts onto the starch-covered paper, completely covering the paper. Let the design dry.
4. Cover your ironing board with paper towels. Place the tissue-paper design on the paper towels, and cover with the remaining sheet of wax paper. Top with another layer of paper towels. Press with a warm iron to fuse the wax paper to the tissue-paper design. Discard the paper towels.
5. Tape the "stained glass" to a window.

Stained-Glass Windows with Crayons

Here's another way to make "stained glass," this time by re-using old crayons.

ages: 4 years and up

prep time:
   20 minutes
skills:
   • manual dexterity
   • design concepts

what you need
• Tape
• 1 piece of cardboard, about 9" × 12"
• 2 sheets of wax paper, same size as cardboard
• Crumbled bits of crayon, or crayon shavings
• Iron and ironing board
• Paper towels

what to do
1. Tape the first sheet of wax paper over a piece of cardboard.
2. Let your child create a design on the wax paper by sprinkling crumbled crayon bits or crayon shavings over the paper.

3. Layer the other sheet of wax paper on top of the design. Tape it onto the board.
4. Carefully lift the cardboard, keeping it level, and place it on the ironing board.
5. Cover the wax paper with paper towels, and press with a warm iron until the wax crayons have melted. Do not use an iron that is too hot, or the crayons will start to smell.
6. Once dry, remove the cardboard. Fold the tape over the edges of the two pieces of wax paper, and then tape the design to a windowpane.

Floating Lily-Pad Game

This game can be played outdoors in a wading pool, in the bathtub, or with a basin on a table.

ages: 4 years and up
prep time: 10 minutes
skills:
• manual dexterity
• eye-hand coordination
• estimation

what you need
- Disposable pie tins
- Green construction paper (optional)
- Plastic wrap (optional)
- Plastic basin, bathtub, or wading pool, filled with water
- Coins or other game pieces

what to do
1. To add a bit of authenticity to the "lily pads" (pie tins), cover the inside of each tin with a circle of green construction paper. If you like, cover the tins with plastic wrap to keep the paper from getting soggy.

2. Float two or more pie tins in the water.
3. Your child can play alone or with a friend. Each player receives a pile of coins or other playing pieces. The object is to toss the "frogs" (the playing pieces) onto the lily pads.
4. Players can keep score, noting how many frogs each player has successfully landed.

 PARENTS ALERT

Always closely supervise children when playing with water. Even small amounts can pose a danger to children under the age of 3. Always closely supervise children when playing with potential choking hazards such as small coins.

extra!

For older kids, another lily-pad game is trying to guess how many frogs (coins) it will take to sink the lily pads. The player whose guess is closest to the actual number wins.

Collage

The more materials your child can
add to this artwork, the better.

ages: 4 years and up

prep time:
  20 minutes
skills:
  • manual dexterity
  • design concepts

what you need
• Piece of cardboard or poster
  board, about 9" × 12"
• Crayons or markers
• White glue or paste
• Variety of photos and/or magazine pictures
• Items to add texture, such as cotton balls, toothpicks, small
  pebbles, bits of leaves and grass, and lengths of ribbon and
  yarn.

what to do
Everyday collage. Suggest that your child collect some pictures and other items to create a scene or abstract work of art
by coloring the cardboard or poster board and gluing the items
on it. For instance, after he colors a scene that includes clouds
and a tree, have him paste cotton balls over the clouds and
real twigs and leaves over the tree drawing.

Special-occasion collage. Collect bits and pieces from a special
day. For example, make a birthday collage with bits of decoration left over from the party, photos of guests, and parts of
cards. Or collect sand and other objects from the beach and
attach them to a drawn beach scene.

Bookmarks

As your child moves from quick-to-read picture books to listening to longer stories, learning to mark her place with a fancy bookmark encourages her both to take good care of books and form a habit of reading. Handmade bookmarks also make great gifts.

ages: 4 years and up
prep time: 10 minutes
skills: • manual dexterity • caring for books • reading

what you need
- Poster board or cardboard
- Paints, crayons, and markers
- Magazine pictures or personal photos, dried flowers, stickers, or other decorations (optional)
- White glue or paste (optional)
- Clear self-adhesive vinyl covering
- One-hole punch
- Yarn or ribbon

what to do
1. Cut a piece of the poster board or cardboard into the desired bookmark shape.
2. Create designs using the paints, crayons, and markers. Or create more elaborate bookmarks by gluing on magazine pictures, photos, dried flowers, or other decorations.
3. Cover the bookmark with clear self-adhesive vinyl and trim the edges.
4. Punch a hole in the top and use some colored yarn or ribbon to make strands or tassels.

Woven Baskets

It would be a shame to toss out those plastic berry containers you get at the grocery store, when instead they could be turned into lovely woven baskets.

ages: 4 years and up
prep time: 15 minutes
skills: • manual dexterity • imagination • eye-hand coordination

what you need
• Yarn, ribbon, or strips of paper, cut into 10" × ¼" pieces
• Tape
• Plastic mesh berry containers

what to do
1. Cover the tip of a piece of yarn, ribbon, or paper with a bit of tape to make it easier to maneuver.
2. Demonstrate weaving this material in and out of the small holes of the container. Weaving can be done from open edge to open edge across the bottom; around one row at a time; or in any pattern your child likes, perhaps creating shapes of hearts or flowers and leaving other parts of the container unwoven. Let your child finish the weaving.

Parachute

Parachute into some fun with this
little toy.

what you need

- Square cotton or silk handkerchief (at least 9" × 9")
- 4 lengths of string, each about
  12"
- 3 metal washers or a small doll
  or action figure

ages: 4 years and up
prep time: 10 minutes **skills:** • manual dexterity • understanding air   and movement

what to do

1. Tie each string to a corner of the handkerchief.
2. Tie the other ends of the strings together evenly, leaving 3"
   or so hanging below the knot.
3. Tie the metal washers, small doll, or action figure to the
   dangling ends of the strings.
4. Let your child crumple the parachute, toss it up in the air,
   and watch it float to safety. Or he can stand on a sturdy
   chair and drop the parachute to the floor.

Magnetic Cars and Raceway

This activity combines the lure of race cars with the magic of magnets.

ages:	5 years and up
prep time:	30 minutes
skills:	• basic physics • understanding magnetism • eye-hand coordination

what you need

- Piece of poster board or thin cardboard, big enough to create a raceway (12"–32" square)
- Markers, paints
- 1" × 2" scraps of poster board, for cars; one for each player
- Magnets; one for each car, plus one for each player
- White glue or paste
- Ruler for each player

what to do

1. Draw a raceway on the poster board or cardboard, or help your child draw one. You may want to make a two-lane track.
2. Glue a magnet to the bottom of each car.
3. Glue a magnet to the end of each ruler.
4. Place the raceway on a flat surface, such as a table or the floor. Slide the rulers, magnet sides up, under the raceway, and place a car on top of each ruler's magnet. Have your child pull the cars around the track by pulling the rulers beneath the raceway. For added challenge, use two cars and race your child around the track.

Glove Doll

Like most families, you probably have a few odd gloves hanging around, waiting to find a mate. If you're willing to give up that quest, turn those gloves into adorable little dolls.

ages: 5 years and up
prep time: 10 minutes **skills:** • creativity • manual dexterity

what you need
- Glove, preferably bright-colored and stretchy, any size (one-size-fits-all stretchies work best)
- Thread
- Sewing needles (large for yarn and small for thread)
- Batting or other stuffing, such as dried beans or rice
- Ping-Pong ball
- 4 yards yarn, in a color contrasting that of the glove
- 3 small buttons
- Scissors

what to do
1. Push the ring finger, inside out, into the glove and sew the hole closed.
2. Fill the remaining four fingers and the palm of the glove about ¾ full with stuffing, leaving the top 2" of the cuff unfilled.
3. Tie off the filled portion of the glove with tightly knotted yarn.
4. Place the Ping-Pong ball, which will be the doll's head, inside the cuff and mark where the eyes, nose, and mouth should be on the outside of the stretched cuff.
5. Remove the Ping-Pong ball, and sew on small buttons for the eyes and nose. Stitch a mouth with yarn.

6. Put the Ping-Pong ball back into the cuff and sew up the top of the glove securely, holding the ball in.
7. Cut about thirty 4" strands of yarn to form the hair. Tie the hair at the center, and sew this wig to the doll's head.

Snow Globe

Your child can shake up a storm with this activity—and you can use those baby-food jars you've been storing.

ages: 5 years and up

prep time:
  10 minutes
skills:
  • creativity
  • manual dexterity
  • understanding the properties of oil and water

what you need
• Hot-glue gun and pellets, or other nonwater-soluble glue
• Small, clean waterproof objects, such as plastic cake decorations or toys
• Small, clean jar with tight-fitting lid and labels removed
• Water
• 2 drops glycerine (available at most drugstores)
• ½ tsp. glitter
• Tape (optional)

what to do
1. Glue small toys or other objects onto the inside of the jar lid. Let the glue dry completely. Be sure that the objects are not wider than the mouth of the jar.
2. Fill the jar with water and the glycerine.
3. Spoon in the glitter.

4. Invert the lid with its attached objects onto the jar. Close the jar tightly. You may want to place tape around the lid to prevent accidental opening.
5. Have your child turn the jar over and watch the glittery snow fall.

Bandana Pillow

Let your child create a Western-motif pillow—perfect for a comfortable reading corner or for lazing on the floor.

ages: 5 years and up	
prep time: 20 minutes	
skills: • creativity • manual dexterity	

what you need
- 2 same-size bandanas
- Straight pins
- Tape
- Chalk
- Ruler
- Sewing needle and thread
- Batting, or a square pillow form smaller than the bandanas

what to do
1. Align the bandanas, right side out, and pin them together. (To avoid getting pricked while working, place a piece of tape over the pointed ends of the pins.)
2. Using chalk, mark a 2" border inside the edges for the seam line. (If you are covering a pillow form, mark a square the size of the form.) The excess material will be the pillow flange.
3. Tie a knot in one end of the thread. Show your child how

to stitch along the chalk line, making at least three stitches per inch.
4. Sew three sides. Remove the straight pins.
5. Have your child insert the pillow or batting and then continue sewing the fourth side closed.

 PARENTS ALERT

Always supervise your child when using needles.

Thing Holder

Does your family always misplace keys? Does your child have a ribbon or ring collection that needs a good organizer? This useful little "thing holder" is a neat project for your child and makes a great homemade gift, too.

ages: 5 years and up

prep time:
  20 minutes
skills:
  • manual dexterity
  • fine motor skills

what you need
• Plywood, about 6" × 2" × 1"
• Sandpaper, fine grade
• Damp cloth
• Ruler
• Pencil

- Paint, crayons, and/or stickers
- 4–6 screw-in cup hooks
- Small picture hook

what to do

1. Sand and smooth the wood, and wipe it with a damp cloth.
2. Measure to evenly space the cup hooks across the piece of wood. Use a pencil to mark four to six spots where you'll place the hooks.
3. Let your child decorate the wood, working his design around the spots where the cup hooks will be inserted. If painted, let the holder dry completely before inserting the cup hooks.
4. Get the holes started for your child by beginning the screwing-in process. Then let your child complete screwing in each hook.
5. On the center of the back, add a small picture hook.

Bank on This!

By kindergarten age, most kids are well versed in the usefulness of money. The desire to save some of it comes naturally right now. Take advantage of that impulse by helping your child make her own piggy bank.

ages: 5 years and up
prep time: 10 minutes
skills:
• creativity
• manual dexterity
• understanding money

what you need

- Clean coffee can with a resealable plastic lid
- Masking tape
- Scissors or craft knife
- Pencil
- Corrugated cardboard
- Pink construction paper, pink self-adhesive vinyl covering, or pink paint
- Black marker
- Pipe cleaner

what to do

1. Check the can for rough or sharp edges; cover any sharp parts with a layer or two of masking tape.
2. Cut a slit in the center of the plastic lid.
3. To make the pig's feet (as a base for the bank), cut two 8" × 4" pieces of cardboard. Center the can on one long edge of one piece, and, using the can as a guide, trace a semicircle onto the cardboard. Cut out the semicircle along the lines and discard the semicircle. Repeat with another piece of 8" × 4" cardboard.
4. Cut a 4" × 1" strip of cardboard. Cut a 1" vertical slit in the center of the bottom of each base, and then slip the bases onto the strip.
5. Cover the can and base with the construction paper and tape or self-adhesive vinyl, or paint them pink. If painting, let dry thoroughly before handling again.
6. Cut shapes for the pig's ears from pink construction paper.
7. Have your child draw a face on the outside of the plastic lid, using the slit as the mouth.
8. Tape the pig's ears to the top of the can. Curl the pipe cleaner into a tail and tape it to the rear of the can.
9. Put on the plastic-lid face and place the can on the base.
10. Deposit a coin into the pig's mouth.

Summer Snowman

So what if the temperature is 90 degrees outside! This snowman won't melt.

ages: 5 years and up
prep time: 15 minutes
skills: • fine and gross motor skills • manual dexterity • creativity

what you need
- 3 white plastic garbage bags
- Newspaper
- Brick or other weight
- String or twist-ties
- Double-sided tape
- Markers
- Snowman clothing, such as a hat and a scarf
- Small tree branches

what to do
1. Let your child fill each bag with crumpled newspaper, creating one large, one medium, and one small filled bag. Place a weight, such as a brick or filled water bottle, at the bottom of the largest bag. Tie off the tops of the bags with string or twist-ties. Cut off and discard any excess plastic from the medium and small bags.
2. Place a piece of tape on top of the large bag and place the medium bag on top. Do the same with the medium bag, placing the small bag on top.
3. Let your child draw a snowman face on the top bag and draw "coal" buttons on the middle bag.
4. Let your child decorate the snowman with a hat and scarf.
5. Pierce the middle bag with two small branches to form the snowman's arms.

PARENTS ALERT

Never let children play with plastic bags or strips of plastic unless closely supervised, to avoid the risk of suffocation. Tie knots in plastic bags or sheets of plastic before discarding.

Paper Snowflakes

No matter what the season, your child will enjoy creating these cut-out snowflakes by himself, with your supervision.

ages: 5 years and up

prep time:
  10 minutes
skills:
  • fine motor skills
  • manual dexterity

what you need
• Plain white paper cut into squares, 4"–8½"
• Scissors

what to do
1. Fold each paper square in half diagonally, in half again, and in half again, making a diamond shape with each piece. Cut an arc across the open end of the diamond, making a cone shape.
2. Cut curved and zigzag notches in the folded and curved edges of each cone. Don't cut close to the cone tip.
3. Open the circle to reveal a beautiful design.

A Very Special Chair

This personalized perch for your child's art corner or for reading will be treasured long after he has outgrown it. Check out your local yard sales for just the right chair, and then choose a good work space for what is likely to be messy a project.

ages: 5 years and up
prep time: 1–2 hours skills: • fine motor skills • manual dexterity • design concepts

what you need

- Child-size wooden chair
- Sandpaper
- Damp cloth
- Gloss or semigloss latex paint, acrylic paint (optional), assorted colors
- Paintbrushes, 2" wide
- Stencil or sponge stamps (optional)

what to do

1. Sand the chair to create a smooth surface. (There's no need to take off the old paint as long as you dull the finish with sandpaper before repainting.) Be sure to remove any dust particles with a damp cloth after sanding.
2. Let your child paint the chair with latex paint. He may choose to paint it all one color or may create a more festive look by painting the legs and/or back slats different colors than the seat.
3. After the undercoat is dry, show your child how to stencil designs or make sponge-stamp imprints in different colors on top of the base layer of paint. He can use acrylic paints for this. (See page 83 for tips on making your own stencils. See page 52 for instructions on making sponge stamps.)

Hand-Holding Paper Dolls

This family of paper dolls really sticks together!

ages: 5 years and up
prep time: 10 minutes
skills:
• fine motor skills
• manual dexterity

what you need
- Plain white paper
- Scissors
- Pencil
- Crayons (optional)

what to do
1. Cut a sheet of paper in half lengthwise.
2. Fold one of the halves, accordion-style, three times crosswise, creating four layers of paper.
3. On the top layer, outline the shape of a person, with head and feet that point toward the open edges and arms that extend so each hand touches a fold.
4. Cut along the drawn outline, leaving the folds uncut at the hands.
5. Unfold the paper, decorate the figures (optional), and say hello to the people.

Paper Beads

Making beautiful jewelry to keep or
to give away is easy with this
magazine-paper beading method.

ages: 5 years and up

prep time:
  30 minutes
skills:
  • eye-hand
    coordination
  • design concepts

what you need
• Color pages from old magazines
• Scissors
• Pencil or chopstick
• White glue or paste
• Thin string or dental floss

what to do
1. From the magazine pages, cut 20 to 30 triangles, each about
   1" at the base and 2" tall.
2. Wrap the base of one of the triangles around the pencil or
   chopstick and begin to roll toward the top point of the triangle. Dab a dot of glue in the middle of the paper each
   time it circles the pencil or chopstick. Continue rolling and
   dabbing until you've rolled the entire triangle. Use one
   more drop of glue to secure the top of the triangle.
3. Gently slide the bead off the pencil or chopstick and lay it
   on a flat surface to dry.
4. Repeat until you've made as many beads as you want.
5. String the beads on the thread or dental floss and tie off.

Soap Sculptures

Here's some good clean fun that can be had in or out of the bathtub. Note that the process of carving soap is slow and requires perseverance. The results are worth it.

ages: 5 years and up

prep time:
  20 minutes, plus
  drying time
skills:
  • manual dexterity
  • design concepts

what you need
- Bar of soft bath soap, such as Ivory
- Pencil
- Plastic knife or wooden craft stick

what to do
1. Unwrap the soap and let it air out overnight.
2. With the pencil, outline any shape, such as a heart or teddy bear, on one wide face of the soap bar. Make the design big so there will be less soap to cut away.
3. Use the plastic knife or craft stick to carve away the soap outside of the pencil marks. Hold the bar as you would hold a potato during peeling and guide the carving tool (slowly) toward yourself.
4. Gather the soap shavings, soak them in a cup for about an hour, drain the water, and remold these leftovers into soap balls or the base for another soap sculpture.

Toothpick Bridge

What makes a bridge sturdy? How does it hold the weight it does? These are the questions kids think about as they design and build their own miniature bridges—and get a physics lesson along the way.

ages: 6 years and up
prep time: 30 minutes, plus drying time
skills: • critical thinking • basic physics

what you need
- 2 stacks of books, each about 2' high
- Wax paper
- Toothpicks
- White glue or paste
- Paintbrush
- Wooden building blocks, or other weights

what to do
1. For the bridge pillars, place the book stacks on a table a short distance apart. For a work surface, lay a sheet of wax paper on the table in front of the books.
2. Lay toothpicks on the wax paper to form a roadway for the bridge. Experiment with different ways of aligning the toothpicks.
3. Glue the toothpicks together; use the paintbrush to spread the glue if you like. Let dry; the glue will not stick to the wax paper.
4. Place the toothpick roadway across the space between the books, and place one block or other weight on top. If the bridge holds, try adding another weight. Continue adding weights until the bridge breaks.
5. Do this activity as a contest. Or make several designs to determine which will hold the most weight.

Thaumatrope

A thaumatrope is a form of moving picture, easy to make and fun
to activate.

ages: 6 years and up
prep time: 20 minutes
skills: • creativity • understanding moving pictures

what you need
- Cardboard round, 4" in diameter
- Pencils or markers
- One-hole punch
- 2 sturdy rubber bands

what to do
1. Draw a picture on one side of the cardboard round, and
   another, related picture, on the other side. (Traditional designs include a bird on one side and an empty birdcage on
   the other, or a dog on one side and an empty doghouse on
   the other.)
2. Punch two holes on two opposite edges of the circle, about
   ½" from the perimeter.
3. Thread a rubber band through each hole, passing one end
   of each loop through the other end to form a slipknot.
4. Holding a rubber band in each hand, rotate the cardboard
   round ten or more times so the rubber bands twist. Continue
   to hold the rubber bands, and let go of the cardboard. As
   the cardboard spins, the two pictures will appear to merge
   and move.

Stencils

Stencils are a great way to see how simple shapes combine to form designs. Before making your own stencils, look through books and/or home-decorating stores with your child to get some ideas. Stencils can be used to decorate wrapping paper or even furniture

ages: 6 years and up
prep time: 15 minutes
skills: • manual dexterity • creativity

and walls. With your help, your child can make these stencils himself.

what you need
- Manila folders
- Pencils
- Scissors
- Masking tape
- Finger-paint
- Small paintbrush or sponge
- Plain paper or other object to decorate

what to do
1. Let your child draw the design he wants on a manila folder with a pencil and carefully outline the border that will be cut out to form the stencil.
2. Before cutting out the stencil shape, cut around the entire design, an inch or so from the edge, to make handling and cutting easier.
3. To cut out the stencil, begin at the outside edge and cut toward the design. Then cut along the outline of the shape to remove it.

4. Tape the cuts in the stencil together so that the stencil will not shift or rip during use.
5. Tape the finished stencil over the item you wish to decorate.
6. Using a brush or sponge, apply paint to any or all parts of the stencil. If your child wishes to use different colors, use a different brush or sponge for each color.
7. When the design is completed, carefully remove the tape and lift the stencil straight up to avoid smudging the paint.
8. If you wish to repeat the design on another part of the object, reposition the stencil. Do not place the edges of the stencil over any painted part of the design that has not completely dried.

Multi-Room Playhouse

Whether it's a fashion doll or a superhero, children love to play with lifelike figures. Let your child create a multi-room home for her dolls or action figures, the likes of which the toy store has never seen. Your child can do this almost completely on her own, but you'll need to cut the doors and windows.

ages: 6 years and up
prep time: 45 minutes or more

skills:
    • manual dexterity
    • critical thinking
    • design concepts

what you need
• Assorted small and medium boxes, such as shoe and shirt boxes
• Pencil
• Scissors or craft knife

- Tape and/or stapler
- Additional cardboard, egg cartons, and/or wood scraps for making furniture
- Fabric
- Markers, paints, and/or crayons

what to do

1. Have your child design the house; explain that each box can be a room, or that boxes can be cut in half or combined. If she needs a little direction, ask questions such as these:
   - What rooms would your doll/action figure like and need in the house?
   - What furniture is needed?
   - How many stories will the house have?
   - How will the doll/action figure walk from room to room? Where are stairways and doors needed?
2. Suggest that your child make a model of the house to see where the doors and windows should go. Have her outline in pencil where cuts are needed. Then do the cutting for her.
3. After cutting away the doors and windows, staple or tape the rooms/boxes together.
4. Supply additional scraps of cardboard, wood, and cloth to make furnishings. Check with a local carpet store for small remnants that can be donated to the cause.
5. Let your child lead the action and decorate and add furnishings as needed.

Tubular Skyscraper

What child can walk past a construction site without stopping to take a look? You and your child can build the skyscrapers your child sees in his imagination with a box of straws and a package of paper clips.

ages: 6 years and up
prep time: 20 minutes to an hour
skills: • critical thinking • basic physics

what you need
- Box of paper clips
- Box of nonbendable plastic straws

what to do
1. Bend the paper clips into S shapes.
2. To connect two straws in a straight line, put one curved end of a clip into one straw and the other curved end of the clip into another straw.
3. To turn a corner, bend an S-shaped paper clip to form a right angle. Then place one end into one straw and the other end into another straw.
4. Form the base of the skyscraper by joining straws to form a square.
5. To build upward, insert a second right-angle paper clip into one straw at each corner.
6. Challenge your child to build a structure that reaches as high as possible without falling down.

Beanbag Dolls

Get in on the beanbag doll craze by making a unique collection of your very own.

ages: 7 years and up	
prep time: 30 minutes **skills:** • Manual dexterity	

what you need
- Fabric, at least 8" × 14"
- Pencil or marker
- Straight pins
- Tape
- Scissors
- Needle
- Thread
- Dried beans

what to do
1. Fold a piece of fabric in half, right side up.
2. On the wrong side, draw the shape of the beanbag doll you want. Choose a simple shape with gentle corners and curves.
3. Pin the two layers together to hold them in place while cutting; be sure to place the pins parallel to the outline so you don't try to cut through them. (Cover sharp ends of the pins with tape to avoid pricking.) Cut through both layers along the drawn outline.
4. Keep the pins in place. Sew around the edges, about four stiches to an inch. Leave an opening in one edge.
5. Turn the shape right side out through the unsewn section.
6. Pour dried beans through the opening until you've included enough to give the doll some form and weight. Don't over-stuff.
7. Sew the opening closed.

Produce a TV Program

Does your child love to make up stories of her own? Or does she have a favorite storybook that she loves to hear over and over again? This activity allows her to transform a beloved tale into a TV program.

ages: 7 years and up	
prep time: 30 minutes	
skills: • Making up stories • retelling stories • putting events in sequence	

what you need
- Ruler
- Sharpened pencil
- Sturdy shoebox
- Craft or utility knife
- Roll of white paper cash-register tape, about 3" wide (available in most office or art-supply stores)
- Tape
- 2 sharpened pencils or chopsticks
- Crayons or markers

what to do
1. Using the ruler and the sharpened pencil, measure and mark a rectangular screen, about 2½" × 3", near the center of one of the short sides of the box. Cut out this shape and save it for Step 3.
2. Cut two holes in the bottom of the box to hold the pencils or chopsticks. Position the holes so that they are just outside the screen area.
3. Unroll a length of the paper tape, but don't cut it yet. Place the cutout from Step 1 onto the paper, about 2" from the start of the roll, and trace around it to form the first "screen." Lift the cutout and continue to outline a series of

screens. After tracing ten or more screens (depending on the length of your child's story), cut the paper about 2" from the last screen.

4. Have your child draw one scene from her story in each screen.
5. Securely tape the beginning of the paper strip to one pencil or chopstick and the end of the paper to the other. Roll the paper around the pencils or chopsticks to tighten it.
6. Place the pencils or chopsticks and paper strip through the holes in the box.
7. To begin the show, wind the paper to reveal the first scene.
8. Have your child retell the story as she turns the pencils or chopsticks to reveal each illustration.

Tie-Dye Shirts

Was tie-dying ever really out of fashion? Kids can make cool shirts for themselves and their dolls using new or old shirts. (Stained shirts can get a vibrant second life with this design method.) It's best to wear old clothes when creating these fashions and, if weather permits, to do it outside.

ages: 7 years and up

prep time:
    30 minutes, plus
    drying time
skills:
    • understanding
      colors
    • design concepts

what you need
• Cotton T-shirt
• Colorfast fabric dye (available at craft and toy stores)

- 2 or more basins
- Rubber bands

what to do

1. Follow the package directions on the fabric dye, and place the cooled dye in a large basin. Have another basin of plain cold water ready, too.

2. To make tie-dye circle patterns, grab handfuls of the shirt and place rubber bands around each. To make a striped pattern, roll the shirt (from top to bottom or side to side, depending on which way you want the stripes to run) and place rubber bands at intervals along the roll.

3. To make a one-color tie-dye, simply dip the shirt in the dye and leave it there for 15 to 30 seconds. Squeeze out the excess water and dye, and dip the dyed shirt into the basin of plain cold water. Then squeeze out the excess again.

4. To make a multicolored tie-dye, dip each part of the shirt into the color you want. Squeeze out the excess water, dip that part into clear, cold water, and squeeze the excess again. Then go on to another section of shirt with another color, again squeezing out the excess and rinsing in cold water.

5. Leave the rubber bands on for about 15 minutes. Remove the bands and rinse the shirt in clear, cold water once again. Let dry flat.

The-Real-Me Paper Dolls

This is a set of paper dolls you and your child will treasure forever.

ages: 7 years and up
prep time: 1 hour, plus photo development time
skills: • manual dexterity • imagination

what you need

- Camera with a roll of 24-exposure film
- 1 page from a self-adhesive photo album, or card stock and glue
- Craft knife or sharp scissors
- Self-adhesive hook-and-loop tape dots (available at most art-supply and stationery stores)

what to do

1. Have your child dress in snug-fitting clothing, such as a leotard. Ask her to stand in a comfortable pose with her arms positioned away from her body and her feet slightly apart. Snap a photo, both front and back, from exactly the same distance.
2. Now have her dress up in various outfits and assume the same pose. Take a picture of your child in each outfit, from exactly the same distance.
3. Have the photos developed and blown up to 5" × 7" or 8" × 12".
4. Cut out the front and back views of your child wearing the leotard.
5. Mount the front-view photo on a self-adhesive photo album page or card stock and cut along the outlines.
6. Attach the photo of your child's back to the other side of the photo album page or card stock.
7. Cut out the various outfits from the rest of the photos.

8. Affix a small loop dot to each shoulder of your child's
   paper doll. Affix small hook dots to the back of each outfit
   photo in the same positions.
9. Let your child dress up her new doll by attaching the hook-
   and-loop dots.

workouts

great ways to get physical

Physical play strengthens not only your child's muscles, but her mind, too. In the art of growing, your child moves from a still life to a mobile in what seems like lightning speed. One day she'll be mesmerized by the discovery of her toes. Not much later she'll be ready to kick a ball across a field. After all, movement is the defining characteristic of childhood. Why be *here*, when you could be *there*? Why *sit*, when you can *run*?

In this section you'll find ways to join in your child's ever-expanding physical accomplishments, helping him reach new levels of competence and confidence.

workouts

Basic active toys

In addition to lots of space in which to run (or crawl) around, your child will benefit from having the following equipment and supplies on hand in order to complete the projects included in this section:

- A variety of balls, including Ping-Pong balls and beach balls; plus balloons (the Mylar ones are safer than latex) and cloth balloon covers (available in most toy stores)
- Riding equipment, such as tricycles, bicycles, and skates
- Targets, including household objects such as laundry baskets and cartons
- Chalk, for drawing sidewalk-game grids
- Jump ropes, hula hoops, and other low-tech toys

Can You Find Me?

There's nothing like the sound of your voice to capture your child's interest—and that's all you need for this activity.

ages: 6 weeks and up

skill:
- listening
- following visual cues

Simply stay by your infant's side, cover your face with your hands or a small blanket and say, "Where am I?," as you reappear. Repeating the activity will delight her as she learns to anticipate the happy "reunion."

For toddlers, let them see you hiding behind an object they can easily approach. Then call, "Where am I?" Invite your older toddler to take turns hiding. Pretend to have just a little difficulty finding her. (Don't take too long, however, or pretend to be too distressed.) Announce your discovery with an enthusiastic, "There you are!"

Find That Sound!

This is a variation of the visual form of hide-and-seek.

ages: 8 months and up

skill:
- listening

For this game, hide a wind-up musical toy or music box while your child is not looking and then let him follow his ears to discover the hiding place as you carry him or follow him around the room.

An older toddler will enjoy a timed version in which he discovers the source of the sound before the music winds down. If you have a number of musical toys and/or music boxes, get them all going, and let him follow the various tunes to their source.

Have a Ball

Infants, toddlers, and older kids, too, will enjoy this slow roll.

ages: 8 months and up

skill:
- balance
- body awareness

You'll need a large ball—about 24" in diameter or larger, that's sturdy enough to support your child's weight. To give your child a ride, gently place her, tummy down, atop the ball. Hold her securely as you roll the ball very gently from side to side. Toddlers and older children will enjoy a more energized roll as they practice balancing.

Magic Carpet

Your child is sure to enjoy this magic-carpet ride through the house.

ages: 14 months and up
skill: • balance

Clear a path and set your toddler on a beach towel or folded blanket, in a tummy-down position. Pull him along the path.

For older toddlers, add a few make-believe destinations to your itinerary—the North Pole in the kitchen, the Old West in the living room—any place your child's imagination wants to take him.

Tunnel Maze

The journey from here to there can be even more exciting when it includes an interesting tunnel pathway.

What you need
• Utility knife
• Large boxes
• Masking tape (optional)

ages: 18 months and up
prep time: 5–40 minutes, depending on the length of the tunnel and the materials used
skill: • spatial skills

what to do

Make a tunnel by cutting two sides from a large box. With your child at one end, go to the other end and call his name. He'll feel a thrill of accomplishment as he makes it through to the other side.

For added fun for older toddlers and preschoolers, make a long tunnel with a series of three or more boxes taped together. Include a turn or two. Cut out a few windows to let in the light, since little kids tend not to like the total darkness of a long tunnel.

Pillow Walk

Soft landings are assured when you cover the floor with pillows.

ages: 18 months and up

skill:
- large muscle development
- balance

Throughout the room, pile bed pillows and sofa cushions around the floor—in some places just one pillow deep, and in other places, two and three pillows deep. Lead your child around the room on all fours, climbing up and down these pillow mountains.

Snacks on a Stick

Even toddlers can safely cut and slice soft fruits and create fruit kabobs for the whole family to enjoy. These can be eaten plain or dipped into chocolate sauce.

ages: 18 months and up

prep time: about 15 minutes

skills:
- eye-hand coordination
- manual dexterity

what you need
- Plastic knife
- Easy-to-slice fruits, such as bananas, watermelon (with seeds removed), cantaloupe, and canned pineapple
- Dull-ended chopsticks
- Serving plate
- Plastic wrap (if kabobs are being served later)

what to do
1. Demonstrate the cutting technique, slicing each fruit into 1" pieces.
2. Help your child place the cut fruits onto the chopsticks, alternating fruits for a colorful effect. (Younger children will need help with this.)
3. Arrange the kabobs on a serving plate.
4. Eat them right away or cover them in plastic wrap for serving later.

Under and Over

This is a follow-the-leader game in which the leader—most likely you—heads around the room or the playground going under and over stationary fixtures.

ages: 18 months and up

skills:
- large muscle development

As you lead the way, announce what you're doing—"I'm going under the table and over the chair"—and invite your child to do the same. If you'd rather not do the climbing and crawling yourself, have your child follow a ball, truck, or stuffed animal that you maneuver under and over the various obstacles.

Bubble Chase

Kids love bubbles. Catching those bubbles and making them burst can get your child giggling and moving.

ages: 20 months and up

skills:
- eye-hand coordination
- gross motor skills

Before beginning the chase, give your child some time to observe bubbles. (Don't be surprised if your baby or toddler gets upset when a bubble bursts; that's a common first reaction.) Use commercially available bubbles and wands or make your own (see page 5 for bubble mix; see page 33 for wand directions).

Find a safe space for running, indoors or on a soft lawn. Start by blowing a few bubbles and encouraging your child to catch them. Then make multiple arcs of bubbles and watch as your child tries to run in different directions at once to capture them all.

With older children, reverse roles and takes turns blowing and catching bubbles.

Bagel Tower

This is a perfect pre-Sunday-brunch activity—before everyone digs into a bag of fresh bagels.

what you need
- Clay
- Plastic wrap
- Dowel
- Bagels

ages: 24 months and up

skills:
- eye-hand coordination
- manual dexterity

what to do
Start with a mound of clay, cover it with the plastic wrap, and stick the dowel into the mound. Show your toddler how to stack the bagels one atop the other on the dowel.

Hug-of-War

Here's a toddler version of big-kids' tug-of-war; the object is to pull your partner close for a big hug. Clearly this is a win-win game!

ages: 24 months and up
skills: • strength development

Use a large bath towel or beach towel. Hold one end and give your child the other end. Each of you needs to grasp your end firmly and pull in opposite directions. Whoever pulls her "opponent" across an imaginary line in the center gets a big hug. Take turns giving and receiving hugs.

Tongs Alot!

Now that your toddler has mastered the fine art of picking up small objects with her hands, offer her this fun challenge.

ages: 24 months and up
prep time: less than a minute **skills:** • manual dexterity • eye-hand coordination

what you need
• Small items, such as Ping-Pong balls and building blocks (small enough to fit into the container compartments)

- Multi-compartment container, such as a muffin pan or an egg carton
- Kitchen tongs

what to do

1. Arrange the items next to the container.
2. Demonstrate using the tongs to lift the objects.
3. Show your child how to place the objects into the container.
4. Discuss how the different objects make different sounds as they land in the container.

 PARENTS ALERT

Be sure that none of the items included will pose a choking hazard.

Balance Beam

This activity helps your child practice keeping her balance and is lots of fun, too.

what you need

- Wooden beam, about 4" × 6' × 2"
- Bricks or sturdy books

ages: 24 months and up	
prep time: 10 minutes	
skills:	
• large muscle development	
• balance	

what to do

1. Check that the beam is free of splinters. Test it to be sure that it's strong enough to support your child's weight.
2. Start with the beam on the floor and invite your child to walk across it.
3. As she gets the hang of walking across it, raise the height by placing the beam on two stacks of bricks or books positioned at each end (one brick high for younger kids, and higher for older ones, making sure the base is sturdy). Then encourage your child to walk the plank.

Jump for Joy

Toddlers love to jump and, with a little ingenuity, you can add loads of fun to this pleasurable activity. Encourage your child to jump into the landing pad from the floor or, holding onto your hand for balance, let her leap from a low, sturdy perch. Some ideas:

ages: 24 months and up
skills: • large muscle development

Create a soft landing. Put an old mattress or pillows on the floor to cushion landings.

Give your child a target. Place a large ring, such as a hula hoop, on the floor for your child to jump into.

Build a hurdle. Give your child small, soft objects (such as stuffed toys) to jump over. Count the number of objects she can jump over.

Join in. No doubt, your child will find this pretty funny.

Ping-Pong Puff Ball

You can play this game on both a dry surface, such as a tabletop, or with a basin of water.

ages: 24 months and up
skills: • oral muscle development

Simply place a Ping-Pong ball on the top of the surface and invite your child to huff and puff and blow the ball across the surface. Toddlers will be quite amazed at their ability to move objects under the power of their own breath. For added fun, join in, taking turns blowing the ball back and forth to one another or setting up a race, using two balls.

Household High Jinks

A variety of household objects easily can be transformed into play equipment to create low-cost, spur-of-the-moment fun.

ages: 24 months and up
skills: • varied

Bathtub bowling. Let your child take a few plastic bowls into the bath and use his strength to push them beneath the surface of the water. It takes more strength than you might imagine. Your child will enjoy the great gush of water that follows this activity. Let him first try to force the bowls under face up, and then face down, which is far more challenging.

Hat toss. Take a few lightweight hats—such as straw hats—and set a broom at an angle, perhaps by leaning it against a chair. Let your child toss the hat onto the broom. Children of different ages can play together if you keep the challenge level fair by raising or lowering the broom.

Bottle bowl. Before heading to the recycling center or back to the store with your redeemable plastic bottles, line them up in a bowling-pin triangle and have your child and his friends take turns rolling a ball to knock over the "pins." For older children, add some difficulty by weighting the bottles with water or sand and securing the tops with bottle caps. A heavier ball will be needed to topple these pins.

Walk Like a Duck

Your toddler or preschooler will get a kick out of trying to waddle like a duck. It's a bit more challenging than it sounds—try it out!

ages: 30 months and up

skills:
- large muscle development
- balance

To do a duck walk, have your child crouch down and hold her ankles, with her arms outside her bent knees. Add some quacking sounds and see how far she can travel before tipping over.

What other animal movements can your child imitate? After she has visited a zoo or viewed some animal-antics videos, invite your toddler or preschooler to walk like a monkey, elephant, horse, or other animal.

Choo-Choo Train

This activity is great for a group of toddlers.

ages: 30 months and up

skills:
- large muscle development

Line up three or more kids, one behind the other, and tell them that they are about to become a train. Direct each child to hold on to the waist of the child in front of him. Tie a long scarf around your own waist so that the first "car" can hold on to you, the "engine."

A toot from a whistle or a chime from a handheld bell is your signal to them to rev up and make their way from room to room. Invite them to use their imaginations as they determine which stops to make—creating a station in the kitchen that they deem to be in the mountains, a stop in the playroom that they designate as the lake, and so on. After the kids get the hang of the game, switch positions, so that everyone gets a chance to be an engine, car, and caboose.

A Hole in One

This is a perfect party game for toddlers and is also lots of fun for just you and your child to play together.

ages: 3 years and up

prep time:
about 15 minutes
skill:
- eye-hand coordination
- taking turns

what you need
- Craft or utility knife
- Large cardboard box
- Markers, crayons, or finger-paints
- Socks or small pouches
- Uncooked rice, beans, or pasta
- Rubber bands

what to do
1. Cut two or more holes in the box top. The holes can be different sizes, but each should be larger than your fist. These are the targets.

2. Have your child decorate the box with markers, crayons, or finger-paints.
3. Make beanbags by filling socks or other soft pouches with rice, beans, or pasta. Secure each pouch with a rubber band.
4. Take turns tossing your beanbags into the targets. Make a game, too, out of retrieving the bags, letting your child collect them between rounds.

Obstacle Course Roadway

Young children's trike and bike adventures are usually limited to flat, enclosed places, and though they thrill at their abilities to pedal, the confined space and

ages: 3 years and up
skills:
• large muscle development

predictable circle path can lose their luster after a while.

Spice up the trail by creating an obstacle course. Simply place beach chairs or other easy-to-maneuver-around objects along the way, and have kids weave in, out, and around these things.

For older kids, add to the fun by placing a ball or other object on each chair and having them pick up the ball from chair 1 and deposit it on chair 2, while picking up the ball from chair 2 to place it on chair 3. The object of this game is to make sure you've placed an item on the chair before the next rider reaches that chair. Kids may want to carry the object in a bike basket rather than grasping it if they find pedaling, steering, and grasping too much of a challenge to handle all at once.

Snake Race

You need just a clear, soft, flat area, such as a tended lawn, for this.

| **ages:** 3 years and up |
| **skills:** |
| • large muscle development |

Have one or more kids lie down with their hands at their sides and slither from Point A to Point B as they pretend to be snakes in the grass.

Island Hopping

Here's a simple, fun way to transform your living-room floor into an adventure at sea.

| **ages:** 3 years and up |
| **skills:** |
| • large muscle development |

what you need
• Tape
• Construction paper

what to do
1. Create "islands" by taping down a few pieces of construction paper around the floor, just far enough apart for your child to step from one to the other comfortably.
2. Announce that the floor is a river and that the only way to cross it is by stepping on the "dry" paper islands.

3. For added challenge, create a few crisscrossing island paths, each made with different-colored paper. Invite your child to get across the river by stepping only on yellow islands, then blue islands, and so on.

Bottom Skating

In this race, your child may well outdo you in natural ability to get from start to finish in a sitting-down position.

ages: 3 years and up
skills: • large muscle development

Set up starting and finishing points and challenge your child—or a group of kids—to a race. The only rule is that each racer must always keep his bottom on the floor.

Five Ways to Use a Hula Hoop

Hula hoops of various sizes can provide hours of active fun.

ages: 3 years and up
skills: • large muscle development

Older children can, of course, try to keep the hoops up as they wriggle and spin. Both younger and older kids also can enjoy these games.

1 **Ready, aim, jump.** Place several hoops on the ground and have your child jump from the center of one into the center of another.

2 **Walk the circle.** Have your child stand inside a hoop and, with his feet, move the hoop across the ground. Set up a few hoops for groups of kids and let them shuffle-race across a smooth floor or play area.

3 **Jump through hoops.** Set the hoop perpendicular to the ground and let it spin or roll as your child tries to jump through the moving circle.

4 **Toss the hoop.** Place an object, such as a plastic soda bottle filled with water, in an open space and have kids try to toss the hoop over it.

5 **Run the hoop.** This is an Early American game that is great for older kids. They'll need a stick (a paint stirrer works well) to play. Holding the stick inside the hoop, kids get it rolling and keep it rolling by running alongside, continuing to hit the inner part of the hoop as they run.

Relay Play

This is a fun race for two energetic kids.

ages: 3 years and up
skills:
• large muscle development
• understanding instructions

what you need
- 2 cardboard boxes or laundry baskets
- 2 different kinds of easy-to-carry items, the same number of each

what to do
1. Set up the cartons or laundry baskets at opposite ends of a room.
2. Fill each container with the same number of different, easy-to-carry items. For example, put six balls in one basket and six stuffed animals in the other one.
3. Have each of two players claim one of the baskets as her own.
4. The object is to get all of the items from the other player's basket into one's own, moving one item at a time. To do this, have the two players stand at the midpoint between the baskets and, at your signal, retrieve an item from the other player's basket and carry it to her own basket. Each player repeats this action until she's transferred all the items out of her playmate's basket and into her own. Each player is a winner as soon as her basket is filled with the other's original collection.

PARENTS ALERT

Be sure that the floor is clear of obstacles before the race begins.

Group Playdate or Party Games

Preschoolers are not highly skilled in group dynamics, nor are they supposed to be. Games that require cooperative interaction can wait. With these games, everyone's a winner:

ages: 3 years and up
skills: • large muscle development

Basketball. You'll need a large soft ball, such as a beach ball, and a laundry basket or two. Have children take turns tossing the ball into the basket. Let each child toss until he has made a basket.

Hand-in-hand dancing. Have children hold hands in a line while music is playing. An adult leads the children as everyone weaves around the room, without letting go of one another's hands.

Freeze. Children move while music plays and then freeze when the music stops.

Pass the picture. The children sit in a circle, and while music plays, pass around a picture of an animal. Whoever is holding the picture when the music stops gets to act like that animal. Keep playing until all children have had a turn. (As the "observing" adult, you can control when the music stops.)

Pool Play for Swimmers and Nonswimmers

Help your nonswimmer get comfortable in the water; let your swimmer try out these additions to her repertoire:

ages: 3 years and up	
skills:	
• large muscle development	

Walk racing. With your child standing in waist- to chest-deep water, invite him to walk from one end of the pool to the other. This offers quite a workout!

Ball sinking. It's not as easy as it looks to get a floating ball underwater. Let your child experiment with various-size balls to see how much force is required to push each one under a few feet of water. Remind her to stand back as the released ball zooms to the surface.

Jump for hoops. Toss a few sinkable hoops into the pool and have your child retrieve them. Have nonswimmers standing in water about waist to shoulder height. Swimmers may be able to retrieve the hoops in water as deep as 6'. Be careful to warn children not to dive off the edge of the pool for the hoops; diving could be dangerous in water less than 10' deep.

Foot fishing. Place an item with an opening large enough for your child's foot to fit inside, such as a sunken plastic bucket or a large yogurt container, at the bottom of the pool in an area about waist deep. Challenge him to lift it, using only his foot.

Under and over. With your child in waist-deep water, have her try to go over and then under a floating raft or other pool toy.

 PARENTS ALERT

Always closely supervise children when playing with water. Even small amounts can pose a danger to children under the age of 3.

Beach-Ball Tether

Tee-ball has nothing on this easy-to-make beach-ball tether.

ages: 3 years and up

skills:
- large muscle development
- eye-hand coordination

what you need
- Rope, 6' or longer, as necessary
- Beach ball
- Sturdy tree limb or other high support for rope
- Plastic bat (optional)

what to do

1. Tie one end of the rope securely around the blow spout of a beach ball. (If the rope is too thick or the spout not quite long enough, connect the rope and spout to each other with a short length of string tied tightly to each.)
2. Secure the other end of the rope around a sturdy tree limb or other support, leaving the ball to dangle at about your child's hip level.
3. Demonstrate hitting the ball with a bat or with your hands and let your child aim and whack.

Play Ball-oon!

Here are some soft alternatives to traditional ball games. For each game, place a balloon inside a commercially made cloth balloon cover (available in most toy stores) before blowing it up. (Broken balloon bits are a serious choking hazard. The cover will give the balloon the necessary extra weight and will reduce the chance of your toddler coming into contact with any broken balloon pieces.) If you can't find a balloon cover, use a beach ball instead.

ages: 4 years and up

skills:
- large muscle development
- eye-hand coordination

Tennis. Hang a bedsheet or other cloth between two chairs to serve as a net. Let two or more players lob the balloon back and forth across the net using their hands or plastic paddles.

Basketball. Secure a lightweight plastic laundry basket just above your child's eye level, and let her aim and fire. Keep the basket low enough for your child to retrieve the balloon safely herself.

Hockey. Set up open boxes (larger than the balloon) on either end of a level, open play space, and assign one as a home box for each player or team. Players can either hit or kick the balloon into their goal box or sweep it in with child-size brooms. The object is to make as many goals as possible while keeping the other side from scoring.

Miniature Golf

Turn any room or backyard into a golf course just right for your child.

ages: 4 years and up	
prep time: 5 minutes	
skills: • large and small muscle development	

what you need
- Boxes, pails, and other containers larger than the ball you're using
- Masking tape, or rocks or other weights
- Child-size broom or hockey stick, or toy golf club
- Ping-Pong ball or other lightweight ball

what to do
1. Lay open boxes, baskets, or buckets on their sides, all over the floor or backyard. The more "holes," the better.
2. On a hard surface, tape the containers to the floor with

masking tape. On grass, place a weight such as a rock inside of each container to keep it stable.

3. Provide your child with a child-size broom or hockey stick,
   or toy golf club.
4. Explain that the object of the game is to sink the ball into
   each "hole." Show your child how to aim and fire.
5. Create additional challenges by placing some obstacles on
   the golf course. For instance, in front of the third hole, place
   a pile of books that your child must navigate her ball
   around in order to reach the target.

 PARENTS ALERT

If more than one child will be playing, explain that kids must
take turns and stand out of the way when another child is swing-
ing.

Carnival Races

Old-fashioned picnic games are a
big hit with little kids. Try these
with your younger child. For kids
over age 5, let them team up with
one another.

ages: 4 years and up
skills: • large muscle   development

Three-legged race. Standing side-by-side with your child, gently tie your left leg to his right leg and hobble your way together toward a predetermined finish line.

Sack race. An old pillowcase works well for this one. Simply invite your child to step inside and hop across a room or a safe outdoor area.

Wheelbarrow race. This one's great for kids who have the arm strength to support their own weight. Have your child lie face down so you can grasp her ankles and gently lift her legs; then have her walk on her hands across the raceway. Walk slowly to avoid any tumbling.

Egg race. You'll need a large spoon and a hard-boiled (or wood or foam) egg. Have your child balance the egg in the spoon and walk as quickly as possible to the finish line without dropping the egg. You can adapt this game for various ages by giving the younger players a larger spoon—even a ladle—and the older players, including yourself, a teaspoon-size holder.

 PARENTS ALERT

Be sure that the raceways are clear of any obstacles.

Sticky Ball

Here is a silly game to play out in the yard with a ball that won't roll away.

ages: 4 years and up
prep time: 30 minutes
skills:
• eye-hand coordination
• manual dexterity

what you need
- Glue or stapler
- Mittens or gloves
- 2 heavy-duty paper plates or cardboard cut into 8"-diameter circles
- Self-adhesive hook-and-loop tape (available at most art-supply and stationery stores), about 3" × 36"
- 1 or more Ping-Pong balls

what to do
1. Glue or staple an old mitten or glove to the back (underside) of each plate or cardboard circle, making sure that your child's hand can slip inside comfortably. (Make both left-handed and right-handed varieties.)
2. Cover the front (topside) of each plate or circle with strips of loop tape placed edge to edge.
3. Trim away excess loop tape, leaving a smooth, rounded finish on each plate or circle.
4. Cover one or more Ping-Pong balls with hook tape.
5. Encourage kids to toss and catch the sticky ball in the plate or circle mitt.

Blow and Go

Who hasn't blown the wrapper of a straw across a room to see how far it could go? These activities let kids see the power of their puffs to move objects.

ages: 4 years and up
prep time: 10 minutes **skills:** • oral muscle development • basic physics • measuring

what you need

- Flat area such as a tabletop or floor
- Masking tape
- Ruler
- Items of different weights, such as a feather, Ping-Pong ball, marshmallow, and plastic or wooden block
- Straws

what to do

1. To figure out how much force is needed to blow different items across a given distance, set up a flat raceway. Use masking tape to mark start and finish lines on a tabletop or the floor. (The lines should be between 1' and 3' apart.) Have your child experiment with blowing different objects from the start line to the finish line. Talk about how the shape and weight of the object made it more or less difficult to blow.

2. To see how wind can control the path in which objects move, create a pathway for your child to follow. With tape, map out a curved course on the floor or table. Blow through the straw to direct an object around the path. Discuss how lighter weights are easier to move but harder to keep on track, while heavier objects take more power to move but are easier to control.

High Walkers

Before beginning, test the strength of the plastic pails, bowls, coffee cans by inverting them and having your child stand on them. They shouldn't collapse or sag.

ages: 4 years and up

skills:
- balance
- coordination

what you need
- Utility knife or awl
- 2 coffee cans or sturdy, flat-bottomed plastic pails or bowls (the same size) that can be punctured
- 2 lengths of rope, each 4'

what to do
1. Punch two holes at opposite sides of each pail, bowl, or can, about 1" above the bottom.
2. Working from the outside across the inside and back to the outside, thread one 4' length through both holes on each pail, bowl, or can, and then knot the ends together at a distance that is comfortable for your child to hold as he stands on the inverted object.
3. Have your child stand on the pails, bowls, or cans, hold a rope in each hand, and step high.

Fly a Kite

A kite, a kid, and a breezy day make a perfect combination.

Set sail with a store-bought kite or make one of these.

ages: 4 years and up	

prep time:
0–15 minutes, depending on the kite chosen

skills:
• large and small muscle development

One-page kite. This is easy to make and fly. Simply take a piece of plain white paper, curl in the two top corners, and staple the corners together, forming a cone-shaped top. Use a one-hole punch to put a hole in the center of this cone shape. Slip a piece of string, at least 20" long (and not longer than 60"), through the hole, loop it, and tie a knot. Tape or staple crepe paper, about 10" long, to the other end to form a tail.

Garbage-bag kite. Cut a diamond shape from a plastic bag, measuring 10" × 16" at the diagonal. Make two double-length plastic straws by pinching the ends of two straws and inserting them into the two others. Tape them together to make a cross. Tape or staple the diamond-shaped plastic over the cross, snipping away the excess straw. Tie a string—at least 48" long (and not longer than 72")—around the cross center and knot it securely. Tape crepe paper—about 10" long—to the bottom point to form a tail.

Sponge Race

This activity for two or more kids is perfect outdoors on a warm day.

ages: 4 years and up

skills:
- hand-strength development

Fill a bucket with water and give each player a same-size sponge and a paper cup. The object is to wet the sponge in the bucket and squeeze out the water into the paper cup. How long does it take to fill each cup? Kids can play as a race against each other, in competing teams, or all together against a clock.

Lacrosse

Play a silly backyard game that you make yourself.

ages: 5 years and up

prep time:
15 minutes
skills:
- gross motor skills

what you need
- 2 empty, clean, plastic milk or water jugs, 1-gallon size, with handles
- Scissors or craft knife
- Tennis ball

what to do
1. Hold each jug upside down at the handle. Cut off the bottoms and then cut the sides diagonally from the corner on

each side of the handle toward the bottom of the side opposite the handle, so that each container looks a little like
a funnel with one tall side.

2. Give each child a funnel and show him how to hold it so
he can catch and throw the tennis ball with it.

3. Let the children toss the ball back and forth with their funnels. Only the funnel—not hands—can be used to catch or
throw.

Categories

Here's a version of hopscotch that
builds aiming and jumping skills
as well as thinking skills.

ages: 6 years and up

skills:
- gross motor skills
- categorizing

Draw a six-box grid with chalk on
the sidewalk. Have your child
think of six different categories for which she and her friends
can likely name things, and write the name of one category in
each square. (Kids may need your help with writing and reading back the names of categories.)

The first player bounces a ball into any box. Wherever the
ball lands becomes her category. That player must then go
from box to box, each time bouncing the ball once while saying the name of something or someone that belongs in her
category. If, for instance, a player's ball first bounces on the
grid marked "TV Shows," she would stand in each box,
bounce her ball once, and name a show. In addition to being
able to name six TV shows during her turn, she must be careful to catch the ball after each bounce and not to let her ball

touch one of the dividing lines on the grid—or she has to start over.

Here's what a grid might look like (your child and her friends may choose any categories they want):

Girls' names	Colors	Teachers
Fruits	TV Shows	Book Titles

smart play

learning and creative play

Every observation and experiment in which your child partakes weaves the fabric of learning. In addition to your guidance, your young learner needs the freedom to explore different materials and the encouragement to test out new ideas without fear of failure.

In this section, you'll find ideas that can help expand your own repertoire of engaging activities—ideas that will spark your child's imagination and help her understand the way the world works. There are also many activities that help your child prepare for and add to the school experience, including language development, math and science activities, and logic and organization games.

Speak in Signs

Long before your child has the
ability to speak in words, he can
use his body language to communicate.

| ages: 6 months and up |
| skills: |
| • learning language |

You can guide him in this form of communication by repeating
gestures as you use the corresponding words. For example,
when you ask if he wants "more" of something, place your
fingers of one hand into the palm of the other hand. Create
different gestures for other routines. Don't be surprised if your
child soon imitates these gestures and makes up some of his
own to communicate what he wants.

Listen Softly

In the course of the day, introduce
your child to the words that describe the sensations she feels.

| ages: 6 months and up |
| skills: |
| • learning language |
| and attributes |

When you wrap her in a blanket,
guide her hand over the cloth and
say, "Soft." When she touches a rough fabric, say, "Rough."
When tasting warm foods, say, "Warm," and so on. It won't
be long before your child learns to associate the words with
each sensation.

Catch the Light

For this, you'll need a prism and a sunny day.

ages: 10 months and up

skills:
- understanding light and colors
- eye-hand coordination
- visual tracking

Hang the prism in front of the window and guide your child to the light on the opposite wall. Let him touch the colors. Stand with him in front of the beams to catch the colors on his own body and yours. Gently shake the prism and watch the colors dance.

Mirror, Mirror

Looking themselves over in the mirror is a favorite activity for most kids. Here's a way to make it even more fun.

ages: 12 months and up

skills:
- self-knowledge

Using washable poster paints, paint a hat, glasses, or a big bow tie on the mirror and position yourself or your child to fit within the drawing. Or, tape a mask onto the mirror and let your child see himself "wearing" the mask by positioning himself so that his eyes or full face are covered by the mask (depending on the size of the mask).

My Turn, Your Turn

Learning to take turns is a major accomplishment for toddlers. Try these games to give your child some playful experiences with turn taking.

ages: 2 years and up

skills:
- sharing
- taking turns
- social skills
- language development

Play ball. As you roll a ball back and forth, be sure to explain, "It's my turn. It's your turn to catch. Now it's your turn to roll and my turn to catch."

Share finger foods. Make a game out of taking turns reaching for slices of banana, french fries, or other finger foods from a shared plate.

Hire a helper. Give your child a turn helping you perform various fun tasks, like putting the quarters in a laundromat machine or opening the mail.

Invite friends. Have a pretend party with your child's dolls and teddy bears, suggesting that your child share a special toy with each. Move on to a playdate with another child, honing your child's sharing skills.

Post Haste

To grown-ups, temporary sticky notes are a great convenience. To your young child, they're nothing short of a miracle. Here are some games your toddler or preschooler will enjoy with the help of those little stick-'ems.

> **ages:** 2 years and up
>
> **prep time:**
>   less than a minute
> **skills:**
> * observation
> * manual dexterity
> * recognizing parts of a whole

Pin the sticky note to a target. Announce a few targets in the room, such as the refrigerator door, a table leg, or any other reachable spot and have your child find and claim that space with a note.

Create a face. Draw face parts on each of five or more notes—two eyes, one nose, a mouth, and maybe a goatee. Have your child arrange them to make a face.

Cover up. Go through a familiar book, covering certain pictures with the notes, and have your child try to recall what's underneath.

Follow the trail. Take turns with your child using notes to mark a trail through the house for the other to follow. For more fun, take turns placing a surprise at the end of the trail for the other to find.

Shape Hunt

Both at home and on outings, you
and your child can play shape-
hunting games.

ages: 2 years and up
skills:
• recognizing and naming shapes

First, help your child learn the
names of basic shapes such as circles, triangles, rectangles,
and squares. Then go on a shape hunt, finding, for instance,
all the circles in your kitchen—the sink drain, the top of a
soup can, the stove dials and burners. Outside circles might
include manhole covers, car wheels, and puddles.

Preschoolers can add some special shapes to their collection
of recognizable symbols—such as the shape of a one-way sign
or a stop sign.

Also, encourage your child to find a number of shapes in
one object, such as round wheels and rectangular doors and
license plates on a car or triangular roofs and square windows
on a house.

Color Search

This is a game for older toddlers
and preschoolers who have some
familiarity with the names of colors.

ages: 2 years and up
skills:
• categorizing
• understanding colors

Choose a color that is well represented in the room. Then have

your child search for all objects or motifs that are that color. For example, if you choose the color blue, he could name your blue shirt, the blue dish on the table, the blue flowers in the wallpaper, and the blue towel in the kitchen.

---

extra!

Make each day a color day. Announce that today is "red" day, and dress your child (and yourself) in red; eat cherries; search for red in the house and outdoors. Tomorrow, pick another color.

What's Your Category?

This game can help your toddler understand similarities between nonidentical objects.

ages: 2 years and up

skills:
- categorizing
- vocabulary building

Choose a distinctive category of objects, such as toy cars. Scatter these around the room and ask your child to point to them or bring them all to you. Or line up about six toys, including two or more toy cars, and ask that he pick out the cars from the larger group of toys.

---

extra!

For older children, or to make the game more difficult, play "beat the clock" by asking your child to find items in the category within a specific amount of time.

Surprise Box

Indulge your child's love of surprises with this special box.

ages: 2 years and up

skills:
- observation
- language development

Decorate a medium-size box by covering it with wrapping paper. As items that might interest your toddler—a broken telephone, a feather, a pretty leaf, a noisemaker—come your way, put them in the box. Whenever you've got three or so new goodies, announce that it's time to peek into the surprise box. Have your child choose one object at a time, and talk with her about where it came from, what it does, how it works. Use lots of descriptive words, talking about its color, shape, and texture.

Silhouette Signs

As your toddler is fast figuring out, things come in many different shapes in addition to round, square, and triangular. There are spoon shapes and glove shapes, and toy-car shapes, too. Help your toddler add new and inter-esting shapes to his visual and oral vocabularies.

ages: 2 years and up	
skills:	
• visual discrimination	
• language development	

What you need
• Pencil
• Small objects with interesting silhouettes
• Plain white paper

What to do
1. Trace the outline of each item onto a separate piece of paper.
2. Place the objects you've traced on a tabletop and line up the tracings.
3. Help your child match the objects to their outlines.

★ Also see "Trace Me" on page 40.

It Feels Like a . . .

Your toddler is just beginning to learn to distinguish objects by touch alone, and this game will sharpen those skills.

ages: 2 years and up
skills: • tactile learning

Find a familiar object with a distinctive shape and texture, such as a spoon, a stuffed toy, a crayon, or a book, and put it in a paper bag. Have your child reach in and handle one object without removing it or looking at it. Ask him to describe it: Is it soft or hard? Is it big or small? Can he guess what it is?

---

extra!

For older children, put a number of similar objects into a bag, such as a crayon, a piece of chalk, and a peppermint stick.

Little Me

Take some of the nostalgia for your child's babyhood, mix it with a baby-size doll or teddy bear, and you've got a personalized keepsake that you and your child both will treasure.

ages: 2½ years and up
skills:
• dressing skills
• observing growth
• nurturing behavior

Instead of discarding your child's outgrown clothes or storing them away unseen, use them to dress up his own cuddly doll or bear. As you help him dress his "baby," talk about that long-ago time when he was new, where and when he wore this outfit, and how much he's grown since then. Older children will enjoy having a few changes of clothing for their doll. As your child plays with his dressed-up doll, be sure to admire his nurturing abilities.

Light Show

Kids light up when they first discover the fun turning on a flashlight can bring. Here are some ideas that can expand the enjoyment:

ages: 3 years and up
skills:
• observation
• understanding light and shadow
• story development

Shadows. Place any object with a distinctive shape in front of a flashlight and let your child see the shadow outline she can make on a wall.

Stars. With the lights in the room turned off, place a colander in front of the flashlight and aim it at the ceiling.

Tag game. Play catch the light by aiming the beam at various places on the floor and having your child (and a friend or two) scamper to catch the beam. Cats enjoy this game, too; your child will laugh to see how bemused his kitty is by the moving light.

Movie. Cut out the shape of a favorite TV or book character small enough to fit over the flashlight lens. Tape it to the center of the lens. Then, turn down the room lights, and aim the flashlight at the wall. Help your child make up a story about the character as she dances across the "screen."

Will It Float?

Help your child learn how a variety of familiar objects take to the water. All you need is a basin. A kitchen sink will do, but a clear

ages: 3 years and up
skills:
• basic physics

plastic bowl that your child can see into is even better. This also is a great bathtime activity.

Fill the basin or tub and line up some familiar objects, such as an apple, a crayon, a toy car, a rubber ball, a paper cup, and a spoon. Before placing any of the objects into the water, ask your child to guess if the object will float or sink. Let her place the objects, one at a time, into the water to test her guess. Help her see the common attributes of things that float (lighter weight, air inside, large surface area) and those that don't float (heavier, no air inside, small). Lead her to observe that some items, such as a paper cup, may float until enough water gets inside, causing them to sink.

---

extra!

Let older kids experiment with shapes that float. For instance, will a tightly rolled ball of aluminum foil float? How about the same piece of aluminum foil shaped into a boat? A ball of wax? A boat shaped from the same ball of wax? Explain that a larger area of the water surface can hold more weight than a smaller one can, thus allowing the boat-shaped objects to float while causing the balls, which concentrate the same weight over a smaller water-surface area, to sink.

Watch Me Grow

In addition to recording your child's height and weight in his medical file—and making a full-size drawing of his body, as described on page 40—these

ages: 3 years and up
skills:
• understanding growth

methods offer a fun way for your child to observe his growth over time.

Make handprints. Once a month or so, make fingerpaint handprints. Date each one, and keep them for comparisons.

Use a prop. Every so often (perhaps on each half birthday) take a photo of your child next to the same item, such as a large teddy bear. What's bigger than your child now will, over the course of time, be quite small in comparison.

Save a haircut clipping. Keep a ribbon around a lock of hair. Compare it every so often to your child's hair now. Is it darker or curlier? How has it changed?

Record your child's early attempts at any new skill. Take a video of the first attempt to ride a trike, play an instrument, write her name, and so on. Take additional videos as she progresses, showing the improvement. Play them back periodically to show how much progress she's made.

Shape-Ups

Making shapes is the perfect follow-up to simply locating and naming them. In addition to drawing various shapes on paper, encourage your child to use other materials to create shapes. For instance:

ages: 3 years and up
skills:
• understanding shapes

Making body shapes. Can he curl himself into a circle? Make a triangle with his legs? Stand on all fours to make a rectangle?

Bending shapes. Pipe cleaners and other small, bendable objects are terrific for giving your child a chance to experiment with forming shapes.

Tracing shapes. Demonstrate tracing by holding an object, such as a paper cup, on paper and tracing around it to form a circle, or around a book to form a rectangle.

Cutting shapes. Preschoolers are able to use child-safe scissors to cut paper into various shapes.

Drawing shapes in nature. A stick on the dirt, a shovel in the sand, or a series of footprints in the mud can form huge shapes that your child can create and then view from a distance.

Big-Kid Words

Little kids love big words. Adding some enormous (huge, gigantic, stupendous, or extravagant) words to her vocabulary is sure to delight your child, from preschool age on up.

ages: 3 years and up
skills: • vocabulary development

Make a game of introducing synonyms for words your child commonly uses. When she says, "Big," say, "and gigantic!"

When she says, "Tired," add "exhausted" to her list of descriptors. Let her know that there can be more than one word to describe an object or feeling. Make a game out of finding as many big-word substitutions as you can.

What Can It Be?

One of the hallmarks of early learning is discovering the usual use of ordinary objects—a bowl is for holding cereal, a sheet is

ages: 3 years and up
skills: • divergent thinking

for covering the bed, a book is for reading, and so on.

While knowing what things were meant to do is handy information, discovering new uses for ordinary objects really gets your child thinking. A bowl, for instance, can also make a wonderfully silly hat, a guide for drawing circles, or a doll boat. A bedsheet can be transformed into an instant playhouse by draping it over a few chairs. A book makes a neat building block, can be propped open to form a triangular tunnel for small cars to zoom through, or can serve as a toy-car ramp.

In addition to finding new uses for everyday objects, give your child lots of experience in creative play by providing playthings that can be anything he wants them to be. A toy cash register, for example, may be difficult for your child to imagine as anything else. But a shoebox can be a toy cash register as well as a car, a fort, a doll bed, a space station, a—well, you get the idea.

What's Missing?

Your kid will love this challenging memory game.

ages: 3 years and up
skills: • observation • recalling visual information

Arrange a number of familiar objects—a spoon, a mitten, and a doll, for instance—on the table. For younger children, have just three or four objects. For older kids, try as many as eight. Ask your child to look at the objects and then, when he closes his eyes or turns away, remove one object, and have him recall the missing item. Give him clues about it if he'd like. Then let him be the one to hide something. Again, increase the challenge by adding rather than subtracting an object (ask, "What's new?") or by placing it facing right instead of left (ask, "What's different?").

extra!

For older children, you can make the game more challenging:

• Use shapes cut from construction paper instead of objects.

• Use the same shape in different colors and ask your child to determine which color was removed.

• Remove more than one item from a group of at least eight items.

What Will Happen?

As your child plays, engage him
in this game of predicting what
will happen and encourage him
to experiment to find out.

For instance, what will happen
if you:

ages: 3 years and up

skills:
- understanding
  cause-and-effect
  relationships

- Remove the bottom block from a tower of blocks? What if
  you put a large block on top of a small one?
- Mix mashed peas and mashed potatoes?
- Mix red and blue finger-paint? Mix yellow and blue?
- Mix soap with water? Mix food coloring with water?
- Put water into the freezer? Put an ice cube into a hot oven?
- Fill a paper bag with water? Fill a plastic sandwich bag
  with water?
- Blow into a straw? Blow into a straw that's in a glass of
  water?
- Blow at a brick? Blow at a piece of tissue paper?

  PARENTS ALERT

Be sure to demonstrate for your child hot, high, or otherwise
nonchild-friendly conditions.

Let's Make Purple

Once they've learned to name colors, kids get a real kick out of mixing paints to form new colors.

ages: 3 years and up
skills: • understanding colors • basic chemistry

Let your child experiment with mixing by placing a teaspoon or two of red, yellow, and blue poster paints on a paper plate.

Suggest that he try mixing any two colors with the teaspoon to see what happens. He'll learn that:

• Red and yellow make orange
• Red and blue make purple
• Blue and yellow make green

---

extra!

For a fun variation on the above activity, try making "water colors." Fill three glasses with water, and use food coloring to make them red, yellow, and blue. Also have on hand a few smaller juice-type glasses. Now use the colored water to create new colors by pouring colors together into the juice glasses. Add red and yellow to make orange, or blue and red to make purple. Hold up a piece of white paper behind the juice glasses to better see the color you created.

Personalized Picture Dictionary

Store-bought picture dictionaries are oftentimes irrelevant to a child's life. There are so many words in these books that it can be difficult for a child to find the one she wants. Now you can personalize a dictionary just for your child.

ages: 3 years and up
prep time: 30 minutes
skills: • word recognition

what you need
- Photographs or cutout magazine pictures of items that are meaningful to your child
- Empty binder-type photograph album with self-adhesive, removable pages
- Paper
- Pen or pencil

what to do
1. Gather photographs of important people in your child's life, such as Mom, Dad, Grandma, Grandpop, and the family dog. Affix these into the picture album, labeling each one with the paper. Print the labels very neatly, using capitals and lowercase letters correctly. Though your child cannot yet read, she'll soon start to associate those particular letter shapes with the pictures they represent.
2. Add two or three words with corresponding pictures to the book each week, putting words that begin with different letters on different pages. Have your child select each week's words so the words are meaningful to her.

3. As the collection increases, rearrange and alphabetize the pages. Mark the top of each page with capital and lower-case letters. You can then use this book to teach letter sounds later on.

All Fall Down

Young children are familiar with how gravity works. Witness the delight of a toddler at tossing things from her highchair to enjoy the predictable splat on the floor. Now that your child is a little

ages: 3 years and up
skills: • basic physics   • vocabulary development

older, she's probably lost interest in this simple activity. But add some new ideas and see what happens. For instance:

Consistency. What happens when your child drops a solid (nonbreakable) object onto the floor? What happens when she pours a liquid? Ask her to describe the differences.

Sound. What sound does the object make? Can she mimic that sound? Does the sound change depending on the landing surface? For instance, does a pebble sound the same landing on solid ground as it does when it's dropped into water?

Speed. Will it bounce? Will it fall quickly or slowly? Does a feather reach the floor faster than a pebble?

Distance. Will it roll like a ball or stay put like a dish towel?

Who Am I?

In this charades-like game, you and your child take turns acting out various animal antics and guessing who each might be.

ages: 3 years and up
skills: • recognizing qualities of various animals

Your child might choose to walk on all fours and growl while you guess that he may be a lion.

Try a verbal variation, giving one another clues about your identity. For example, you might say, "I live on a farm. I give milk. I say, 'Moo.' Who am I?" This game is also a perfect follow-up to a zoo or farm visit.

Preschool Placemats

Your child will be proud to eat off his new placemat and you can enjoy knowing that he is learning while he eats. Just jazz up the placemat with anything you want to teach. Here's how:

ages: 3 years and up
prep time: 20 minutes   skills: • manual dexterity   • recognizing shapes, numbers, letters, words, and so on

what you need

- Cardboard or heavy paper cut in the desired size and shape of the placemat
- Markers, crayons, paints
- Clear self-adhesive vinyl covering
- Scissors
- Construction paper (optional)
- Glue
- Cutouts from magazines, photographs, and paper souvenirs (optional)

what to do

To construct a basic placemat, allow your child to decorate the cardboard or heavy paper with the markers, crayons, or paints, and then you can place clear self-adhesive vinyl over the front and back. Use any of the following ideas, or any others that occur to you.

Shape teacher. Cut out different geometric or letter shapes from the construction paper and glue the cutouts around the placemat perimeter. Lay out geometric shapes in a pattern, teaching both patterns and shapes. Arrange letters in alphabetical order.

Dictionary mat. Glue favorite pictures, such as a train and car, on the placemat, and write their names under each picture, creating a picture dictionary mat.

Memory mat. Collect photos and paper souvenirs—such as ticket stubs, napkins from restaurants, sections of maps—from a vacation and arrange these on the mat. Encourage kids to recall their adventures.

Place-setting guide. Once your child is old enough to help set the table, this mat will come in very handy. Draw or collage a plate, glass, napkin, and silverware in its proper place as a guide for your child to copy.

A Word to the Wise

If you've ever tried to skip a page in your child's favorite storybook, you know that she's memorized the passages, word for word. Turn that skill into a fun game the

ages: 3 years and up
skills:
• predicting
• memory skills

next time you pick up a very familiar book.

Read a passage but leave out a word, and have your child provide it. She will especially like announcing last words on a page, particularly ones that rhyme with a word you've already read.

Count on Me

Preschoolers are amazed at all their bodies can do, so teaching simple math with their bodies is a great way to introduce numbers and reinforce number concepts.

ages: 3 years and up
skills:
• number sense

Start by having your child count on his body:

- 1 head, 1 nose, 1 belly button, 1 tongue
- 2 hands, 2 arms, 2 elbows, 2 legs, 2 feet, 2 knees, 2 eyes, 2 ears

- 5 fingers on one hand
- 10 fingers, 10 toes
- How many teeth? How many freckles?

Then count how many times he can do 10 jumps, 3 hops on one foot, etc.

Make Color Rain

Watching heavier food coloring fall to the bottom of a glass of water looks like magic. And it is.

ages: 3½ years and up

skills:
- understanding colors
- comparing the weight of water and another liquid

what you need
- Straight-sided clear drinking glass
- Water
- Food coloring

what to do
1. Fill the glass with water.
2. Help your child put a drop of food coloring on the top of the water. Watch how the color falls in strands to the bottom.
3. Add different colors to the glass of water and observe the effect. What happens when several drops are added at one time?

Letters of the Alphabet

It is sometimes difficult for young children to distinguish between letters of the alphabet. You can help by providing cutout letters to touch, since the sense of touch is often more acute than sight and sound in young kids.

ages: 4 years and up	
prep time: 15 minutes	
skills: • letter recognition	

what you need
- Scissors
- Sandpaper

what to do
1. Cut out letters of the alphabet in sandpaper. Perhaps start with the letters in your child's name if you don't want to do the whole alphabet right now.
2. Encourage your child to manipulate each letter, finding similarities and differences among them.

Letter Sounds #1

Learning the relationship between the look of letters and the sounds of letters is a prereading skill that your child will enjoy learning. To involve a number of senses in this learning, make letter cards or letter shapes that present letter sounds in a tactile way.

> **ages:** 4 years and up
>
> **prep time:**
> 1 hour
> **skills:**
> - letter recognition
> - letter-sound relationships

Your child can glue objects that have the same sound as the letter to the letter shape, or you can make cutouts of each letter with a material whose name begins with that letter. For example, make an *A* out of apple seeds, and a *B* with beads or butter, and so on:

C   out of candy or cookies

D   with dirt or a picture of donuts

E   with erasures (pencil-in a whole page and erase an **E** shape)

F   from finger-paint

G   from a garland

H   from hay or a strand of hair

I   out of ice-cream sticks

J   from juice or Jello

K   from Kix cereal or kazoos or keys

L   from leaves or lollipop sticks

M   from mud or macaroni

N   from noodles

O   out of onions

P   out of paper or paste or pebbles

Q   out of quilt material

R   out of rice or rope
S   in sand or sandpaper
T   out of tape or tea bag string
U   with an old umbrella handle
V   out of velvet
W   out of weeds or wax or watercolors
X   that looks like an explosion
Y   out of yellow yarn
Z   from zippers

Letter Sounds #2

Make learning the alphabet special. Dedicate each day to a different letter.

On *B* day, for example, your child could find as many objects as he can that start with the letter *B*. Wear a belt. Eat blueberries and

ages: 4 years and up
prep time: 5 minutes a day skills: • letter recognition • letter-sound   relationships

beets. Go through magazines and find as many pictures as you can that start with *B*. Create a letter book, and each day write the letter on the top of a page of loose-leaf paper and tape on a few magazine pictures of objects that begin with that letter.

What's My Letter?

Silly sentences help kids remember letter sounds.

ages: 4 years and up

skills:
- recognizing initial letter sounds

"Mommy, monkeys, milkshakes, and mailboxes all have me in front. What letter am I?" Making up silly alliterations is just plain fun and has the added benefit of familiarizing your child with letter sounds. Try starting with the first letter of your child's name—then string along as many words as you can that begin with that letter: "Lucy likes licking lime lollipops. What letter am I?"

What Will Water Do to It?

Let your child experiment to see how water affects various objects, saturating and changing some, while leaving others unchanged. For instance:

ages: 4 years and up

skills:
- basic physics
- understanding the properties of various objects and water

- A piece of tissue paper will absorb the water; it can be dried but will be changed.

- A spoon will not absorb water; wet or dry it retains its shape and form.
- A teaspoon of flour or powdered gelatin will mix into the water and cannot be returned to its original form. In this case, the object changes the water, too.

Keep playing, observing what will happen to cooking oil, to a sponge, or to a piece of cloth when moistened.

Hunt for Treasure

Create a map of your child's room. Then hide something in there and mark an "X" on the map to indicate the location of this "buried treasure." See if your child can find it.

ages: 4 years and up

prep time:
1 hour

skills:
- measuring
- mapmaking
- plotting points on a map
- critical thinking

what you need
- Yardstick or tape measure
- Pencil
- Graph paper

what to do
1. Measure the length and width of the room. Draw the floor-plan on the graph paper, using each box as 1 square foot.
2. Next measure things in the room, such as the bed and dresser, and draw them on the graph paper as well, in scale to the room.
3. Have your child leave the room, and hide an item(s) in

the room. Put an "X" on the map to indicate where it is hidden.
4. Ask your child to locate the item(s) using the map.
5. Change places. Have your child do the hiding and you go on the treasure hunt.

Let's Talk

Forget walkie-talkies. Try these low-tech wonders.

ages: 4 years and up

prep time:
15 minutes
skills:
• understanding how sound travels

what you need
• Garden hose
• Duct tape
• 2 funnels

what to do
1. Take a long garden hose and tape a funnel to each end.
2. Have your child talk into one end while you or a friend listens at the other end. Be careful not to crease the hose or the sound will not travel through it.

---

extra!

Try setting up a silly communication system. If you live in a two-story house, string the hose through windows from the second floor to the first floor, or try looping it out one bedroom window and into the next. If you have a really long hose and a good friend living next door, use the hose to connect both houses.

Paper-Cup Telephones

Even less high-tech and just as fun is the papercup-and-string telephone. This oldie but goodie is still as magical as it used to be.

ages: 4 years and up
prep time: 15 minutes
skills: • understanding how sound travels

what you need
- Finishing nail or unbent paper clip
- 2 paper cups
- String, about 24"–48" long

what to do
1. Using the nail or end of the paper clip, punch a small hole in the middle of the bottom of each paper cup. Discard nail or clip.
2. Thread each end of the string through one cup so the open ends of the cups face the ends of the string.
3. Tie a knot inside each cup to secure the string. Pull the cups taut. Have your child talk into one end while you or a friend listens at the other.

Measure Me

Children are always proud of
how big they're getting. Why not
measure various parts of their
bodies to prove just how big they
are? Specific measuring depends
on the age. For children age 4
and under, measure to the inch;

ages: 4 years and up

prep time:
    about 20 minutes
skills:
    • linear measurement
    • estimation

for older children, measure to the half- or quarter-inch.

what you need
- String, at least as long as your child
- Markers, crayons
- Chart for making notes
- Ruler or tape measure

what to do
1. Have your child use a piece of string to measure her height
   or the length of her leg, her thumb, or other parts of herself.
2. Estimate the length of the string in inches, and write the
   results on a chart, under the heading "Guesses."
3. Measure the same parts of the body, with a ruler or tape measure, and record the results under the heading "Actual Sizes."
4. Compare to see if each guess was higher or lower than the
   actual number.

 PARENTS ALERT

Always closely supervise children when playing with lengths of
string or ribbon to prevent strangulation.

Connect-the-Dots

At the drop of a hat you can play connect-the-dots! Turn to this activity whenever—and wherever—you need to keep your child occupied for short periods of time. If you see that she is quick to complete a picture, set up another of greater complexity.

ages: 4 years and up

prep time:
  5 minutes
skills:
  • putting numbers in
    sequence
  • fine motor skills

what you need
- Plain white paper or tracing paper
- Picture of a simple image, drawn or in a book
- Pencil

what to do
1. Place the paper over the picture. Mark dots on the paper at intervals to correspond to the basic outline of the image of the picture beneath. Use 10 to 20 dots, depending upon the age of your child. Number the dots so that when connected consecutively the outline of the image will be revealed. Remove the picture.
2. Hand the pencil to your child and let her connect the dots.

Paint Factory

Try these experiments to change ordinary poster paint into something new and exciting.

ages: 4 years and up
prep time: 5 minutes **skills:** • creativity • basic chemistry

what you need
- Flour, corn syrup, sand, sawdust, liquid soap, Epsom salts
- Poster paints in a variety of colors

what to do
1. Ask your child what she thinks will happen when you mix each new ingredient into the poster paint.
2. Test her ideas by adding just a pinch of each ingredient to a few teaspoons of paint. Increase the quantities of the additions to observe more changes.

Here's what you and your child will discover:

- Flour creates a lumpy, thick paint with a duller color than the original.
- Corn syrup makes the paint very sticky and shiny.
- Sand and sawdust add interesting textures.
- Soap makes the paint look and feel greasy.
- Epsom salts add sparkle.

After experimenting with mixing, let your child dab some of each new paint on a piece of paper to see how it works in paintings and how long each type of paint takes to dry. (The syrup and soap mixes will not dry completely unless applied in a very thin coat.)

So Big

How many teddy bears tall is your child? In addition to standard measurements of inches or centimeters, let your child know that he can use any handy object as a measuring device.

ages: 4 years and up
skills: • measuring with nonstandard tools

Help him find out by comparing his own height to the height of one or more teddies or other objects. There are a number of ways to do this:

Teddy bears. Have your child stand against a door frame; mark her height with a pencil line above her head. Hold her teddy bear up to the same door frame and mark its height from the floor. Then, placing teddy's feet at this line, measure her again and again until you've reached the height mark of your child.

Blocks. Again, measure your child's height against a door frame. This time, use building blocks to create a child-size tower. How many blocks tall is he?

Cars. For a change in perspective, have your child lie down and line up as many toy cars or other objects as are necessary to match her length.

Mystery Items

You can use this activity to teach and reinforce a number of skills, including alphabet sounds and number sets. Meanwhile, your child enjoys the satisfaction of solving a mystery.

ages: 4 years and up
prep time: 5 minutes
skills:
• critical thinking
• understanding attributes
• categorizing

what you need

- Brown paper lunch bag
- Sets of 4 items that share an attribute you can discuss with your child, such as:
- **"B" things:** book, block, box, button
- **Bathtub things:** toy fish, toy boat, washcloth, bar of soap
- **Round things:** ball, lollipop, button, coin
- **Things that mark time:** watch, kitchen timer, egg timer, calendar

what to do

1. Place one of the items in the bag, keeping the remaining items hidden.
2. Let your child feel the object inside the bag but not look at it. Ask him to guess the item's identity.
3. Once the item is identified, ask your child to cover his eyes while you remove and replace it with a second item in the set. Do this until all four items have been guessed.
4. Show your child all of the items and see if he can guess what feature they have in common.

Toothpick Alphabet and Shape Maker

A box of toothpicks can provide hours of fun for your child.

ages: 5 years and up
skills: • letter and shape recognition

In addition to forming letters and shapes, your child can spell out her name, write messages, and create stick drawings to accompany the words. Using glue, she can also create three-dimensional shapes such as cubes and pyramids.

Make a Volcano

Here's a fun use for baking soda.

ages: 5 years and up
prep time: 15 minutes skills: • basic chemistry

what you need
• 3 Tbs. baking soda
• Tall, thin drinking glass
• ½ cup vinegar

what to do
1. Put the baking soda into the glass. Place the glass in a deep bowl or in the sink—the volcano can get messy.
2. Have your child pour the vinegar into the glass.
3. Stand back and watch the "eruption."

Make a Magnet

What could be more magical than a magnet? Here your child can make her own all by herself.

ages: 5 years and up
prep time: 15 minutes
skills: • understanding magnetism and electricity

what you need
- Copper wire, 2' long
- Steel nail
- Flashlight battery
- Paper clips or other metal objects

what to do
1. Hold the middle of the wire near the tip of the nail. As tightly and as many times as possible, wrap the wire around the nail.
2. Place the ends of the wire against opposites ends of the battery. As long as the wires remain touching the battery, the electricity running through the nail will cause the nail to become magnetized.
3. Test the magnet on some paper clips or other metal objects.
4. To eliminate the magnetism, remove one of the wire ends from the battery.

Now You See It, Now You Don't

With this trick, your child will be able to write with invisible ink.

ages: 5 years and up
prep time: 15 minutes skills: • basic chemistry

what you need
- 2 Tbs. baking soda
- 2 Tbs. water
- Small cup or bowl
- Cotton swab
- Plain white paper

what to do
1. Mix the baking soda and water in the cup or bowl.
2. Dip the cotton swab into the mixture and draw a picture or write a message on the paper. It takes a moment for the mixture to be absorbed; when it dries, a powdery white film can be seen.
3. Trade secret messages with your child.

Tangrams

Tangram designs help your child see shapes in a whole new way. If your child enjoys this activity, make it from felt instead of paper, and have her arrange the pieces on a large felt background—she'll be amazed at how easily they stick together.

ages: 5 years and up
prep time: 5 minutes
skills:
• shape recognition and creation
• critical thinking
• design concepts

what you need
- Pencil
- Construction paper, one color only
- Scissors

what to do
1. Duplicate the diagram on the next page on the construction paper and cut it apart to create the variety of shapes shown: triangles, squares, parallelograms, and so on. If you'd like large pieces, place several sheets of paper side by side when you duplicate the diagram.
2. Encourage your child to replicate the designs shown and to create additional designs of her own.

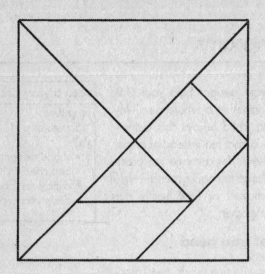

Shadow Theater

Learning to create shadow figures on the wall is a skill your child will hone throughout his life.

All you need for this is a flashlight and a plain wall. Take turns with your child holding the flashlight and creating the shadow images. Or, prop up the light so you both can perform.

See if he can make up some originals. Also, check with the library to find books that include dozens of additions to this "handy" menagerie.

ages: 5 years and up

prep time:
10 minutes

skills:
- creativity
- understanding light and shadow

Today's Word Is . . .

Add this activity to the breakfast menu.

ages: 5 years and up
skills:
• vocabulary development

Have your child open a children's dictionary to any page and randomly point to a word. That's the word for today. Read the word and the definition. Take turns trying to use the word in a sentence.

Throughout the day, try using the word in your conversations.

Hot (and Cold) Air Balloons

Here are two activities that combine the fun of balloons with the magic of physics.

ages: 5 years and up
prep time:
15 minutes, plus waiting time
skills:
• basic physics

what you need
- Round and long balloons
- Empty plastic soda bottle
- Masking tape

what to do

1. Partially blow up a round balloon, but do not tie it closed.
2. Slip the opening of the balloon over the top of the soda bottle, pinching it so that no air escapes. Tape the balloon over the neck of the bottle securely.
3. Ask your child to predict what will happen when you put the balloon/bottle in the freezer. Try it and see. (When the air in the bottle is chilled, the balloon deflates.)
4. Ask her to predict what will happen when you put the bottle into a pan of hot (not boiling) water. Try it and see. (When the air is heated, the balloon inflates more.)

 PARENTS ALERT

Children under 6 playing with balloons must always be closely supervised. Children should never play with broken balloon pieces, which pose a serious choking hazard.

Sound-Effects Stories

Back in the days when radio reigned as the top form of entertainment, there was a sound-effects person who made the required noises to accompany the many audioplays. Why not transform your home into a sound studio?

ages: 5 years and up
prep time: 15 minutes **skills:** • critical thinking • understanding sound • story enhancement

what you need
• Story with sound-effects potential
• Various objects from around the house

what to do
1. Read a favorite story with your child and discuss the sounds that you might hear if you were the characters in the book.
2. Find various items around the house that may make the sounds required. Note that sounds may be made by unexpected items, and may require hard thinking and experimentation to work out. (For instance, you can reproduce the sound of rain by turning over a paper bag filled with uncooked rice; the sound of water dripping can be made by shaking a pliable piece of tin. Try hitting two wooden blocks together to make the sound of horse hooves hitting the trail.)
3. Read the story slowly while your child makes the sound effects.

---

extra!

If you discover some great sound effects that don't fit your chosen story, encourage your child to narrate an original tale.

Haiku Drawings

Haiku is a kind of poetry/parlor game in which each participant contributes a line of a certain meter. The results are often amazing, as each person's individual contribution connects with others' ideas to form something altogether new.

ages: 5 years and up	
prep time: 10 minutes	
skills:	
• creativity	
• collaboration	

In this drawing game, each participant—two or three people can play—contributes a part to a drawing without benefit of seeing the other contributions. Like the poetry, this can have some funny and surprising results.

what you need
- Plain white paper
- Pencil or crayons

what to do
1. Fold a sheet of paper widthwise, accordion style, into thirds.

2. Ask the first player to draw the head of a character—either a realistic drawing or any made-up creature such as a monster or alien. The player should extend the neck part of the drawing into the second section of the paper.
3. The first player then folds back the part he has drawn so that the second player sees only the neck portion on the second section. This player then draws the torso. He should extend the torso of the drawing into the third section of the paper, so that the next drawer knows where to place the legs.
4. The final player (either a third child or the first one again) adds the legs. He then pulls open the paper to reveal the result of the collaboration.

Calendar Games

A monthly calendar can be a game board for a host of activities. For instance:

ages: 5 years and up
prep time:
5 minutes
skills:
• knowledge of
calendars
• number review
• critical thinking

- Reviewing the names of the days of the week
- Counting from 1 through 31
- Marking holidays—both public and personal—and counting down to special occasions
- Playing grids. One player says, "My date is three across and four down," for instance, and the other player names the date.

What Is That We're Eating?

If you have trouble persuading your child to eat his fruits and vegetables, here's a fun way to do it. This is not as easy as it seems, but it is silly and fun.

ages: 5 years and up

prep time:
5 minutes
skills:
• critical thinking
• using clues

what you need
• Blindfold
• Various foods cut into bite-size pieces, such as a pear, potato, broccoli, apple, sweet potato, onion, and carrots

what to do
1. Place the blindfold over your child's eyes.
2. Place a piece of food into his mouth and have him guess what it is.

Pizza as Brain Food

Making homemade pizza is a treat in itself. Add some education to the ingredients with these ideas. Just start with frozen pizza dough and all your favorite ingredients. Then try one of the following:

ages: 5 years and up

prep time:
30 minutes
skills:
• varied

Pizza map. Look at a map of the United States or other large landmass and shape your pizza dough to match the outline. Let kids enjoy taking a bite out of Florida or putting extra olives over their own hometown.

Handprint pizza. After your child has thoroughly washed and dried her hands, sprinkle a little flour on them and have her press them into the dough. Fill the depressions with pizza ingredients.

Divide and conquer. Help your child figure out how to divide the dough and other ingredients into halves, thirds, and quarters to make smaller pies.

Shapely pizza. In addition to traditional pizza in the round, let your child make pizza triangles, pizza trees, or other shapes.

Memory Card Game

All you need for this memory game is a partial deck of traditional playing cards or some index cards and a pen or marker.

ages: 5 years and up
skills:
• memory development

Create 10 to 12 pairs of cards. Lay them, face down, on the table in a grid and take turns with your child trying to match pairs.

The first player turns over two cards. If they match, she keeps the pair and goes again. If they don't match, she turns them back over, placing them in the same spot from which she took them. The next player has an advantage because she's already seen two of the cards. That player then turns over a card. If it matches one that was turned over by the last player and she can recall where it is, she makes a pair, keeps them, and goes again. The players keep playing until all the pairs have been matched.

When playing with your child, be sure to take turns winning. Also, as you play, teach your child the strategy of turning over a card she is unsure of before turning over a just-looked-at card.

Shape Card Game

Try these creative new uses for playing cards!

ages: 5 years and up
skills:
• shape formation

Place about 20 cards from a standard deck—10 black and 10 red—face up on a table. Ask your child to arrange the cards so that he forms shapes with each of the colors. For example, have him lay the cards out in two squares, one black and one red. Then have him make a red triangle within a black rectangle, and so on.

What's in a Name? Personality!

Children love to see their names in print. Here is a way to compliment your child while using her name.

what you need
- Pencil
- Paper
- Markers, crayons

what to do
1. Print your child's name down the side of the paper in capital letters.
2. With your child's help, think of an adjective beginning with each letter that describes your child.
3. Using the capital letter of the name as the first letter, write each adjective across the paper.
4. Decorate the page to reflect the adjectives.

**The name
CAITLIN
might render the
following:**
> Cute
> Artistic
> Imaginative
> Terrific
> Lovable
> Intelligent
> Nice

What's in a Name? Categories!

Here's a name game to sharpen your child's ability to categorize.

ages: 5 years and up

skills:
- vocabulary development
- recognizing initial consonant sounds
- categorizing

what you need
- Pencil
- Paper
- Markers, crayons

what to do
1. Print your child's name down the side of the paper in capital letters.
2. With your child's help, think of a category such as foods, games, or book titles. Then, think of an item in the chosen category that begins with each letter of the name.
3. Using the capital letter of the name as the first letter, write the word for each item across the paper.
4. Decorate the page to reflect the category.

The name
ASHLEY
might render the following:

Apples
Spinach
Hotdogs
Lettuce
Eggs
Yogurt

Can you and your child create a dinner menu named for her?

Same Name, Different Use

Learning to think of different uses for common objects really stretches your child's imagination—and hones her problem-solving skills.

ages: 5 years and up
skills: • critical thinking

Think of an object and its normal use. A glass, for example, is normally used for drinking. Invite your child to think of as many additional uses for it as she can, which might include:

- Device for listening through walls
- Dough roller
- Circle tracer
- Miniature fishbowl
- Paintbrush bathtub
- Musical instrument for tapping

Same Name, Different Meaning

Playing this game will help your child really pay attention to word sounds and meanings.

ages: 5 years and up
skills: • critical thinking • language   development

Pick a word that can have multiple meanings and encourage your child to think of other such words. This list can get you started:

- Trunk (of an elephant/luggage/of a tree)
- Pipe (in plumbing/in a musical instrument/smoking device)
- Ball (dance/something to bounce)
- Bat (rodent/baseball equipment)
- Rose (flower/got up)

What's Inside?

Children's natural curiosity leads them to want to know what's inside all the gadgets they see around the house.

ages: 5 years and up
prep time: depends on how resourceful you are
skills: • prediction • curiosity

You can help them satisfy their curiosity, while giving an old machine a new life as a toy. Take computers, for example. Using some ingenuity, it is not too difficult to find an old computer or printer that is considered worthless by those lacking your child's imagination. You may have one in your basement that you keep simply because you cannot believe something you paid so much for just a short while ago is obsolete already. Or you may put an ad in the local penny-saver for a donation to your cause. At any rate, haven't *you* always wondered what's inside?

what you need
- Assortment of screwdrivers and pliers
- Old computer, printer, or other machine

what to do
1. Using your tools, help your child open the machine.
2. Let your child take the insides apart.
3. If you have the manual that accompanied the machine, see what each of the parts did.

 PARENTS ALERT

Before exploring the inside of any machine, unplug it. After unplugging it, cut off the wire to assure that the rearranged insides cannot be reused.

Pattern Necklace

Create a lovely necklace using color patterns. Tell your child that patterns are a group of anything that repeats in the same way again and again, such as dog, cat, dog, cat, and so on.

ages: 5 years and up

prep time:
15 minutes
skills:
• understanding patterns
• eye-hand coordination

what you need
• Yarn or elastic cord, 18" long
• Tape
• Colorful beads, wood or plastic, large enough to slide onto the yarn or elastic

what to do

1. Cover one end of the yarn or elastic with a small piece of tape to make slipping it through the beads a bit easier.
2. Allow your child to arrange the beads on the yarn or elastic in a repeating pattern, such as red, yellow, blue, red, yellow, blue.
3. As your child masters the idea of patterning, offer her some challenges, such as patterning four or five colors together, such as red, red, red, blue, yellow, green, red, red, red, blue, yellow, green.

Color Lights

Up to three "scientists" can experiment with these colorful beams,
so if your child has friends or sib-
lings, stand aside once you've as-
sembled the lights.

ages: 5 years and up
prep time: 10 minutes
skills: • understanding color and light

what you need

- Scissors
- 3 balloons, 1 each red, yellow, and blue
- 3 flashlights of the same strength
- 3 heavy rubber bands
- White wall or sheet of paper

what to do

1. Cut the tops off the balloons, making three latex circles. Immediately discard the rest of the cut balloons.
2. Place one circle on the top of each flashlight, stretching it over the light and securing it with a rubber band.

3. In a lighted room, let your child shine each light on a white surface, either a wall or piece of paper. Then aim the beams so that the colors overlap. What do you see? The combining colors will make new colors.
4. Repeat the experiment in the dark and see if there is a difference in the results.

 PARENTS ALERT

Children under 6 should be supervised when using balloons, which are a choking hazard. As an alternative, consider using colored plastic wrap.

Home Store

In addition to learning the values of different coins for its own sake, learning to add with money is an interesting way to learn to count by 1s, 5s, 10s, and even 25s.

ages: 5 years and up

skills:
- understanding coin values
- adding

To get your child in the swing of this game, play pretend store, placing price tags on some of his favorite toys. Have your child group coins in various ways to come up with the total price for each toy. For example, if you mark a favorite truck 50¢, your child can count out 50 pennies, 10 nickels, 5 dimes, or 2 quarters, or other combination of coins.

---

extra!

When your child's room begins to resemble the stockroom at the toy store, consider holding a real toy sale, which accomplishes some important things:

- Cleaning out unused and outgrown toys

- Raising money

- Teaching your child to negotiate, count change, and handle customer relations

---

Shape Maker

This low-tech toy can provide hours of creative play and practice making all sorts of shapes.

ages: 5 years and up
prep time: 30 minutes
skills:
• manual dexterity
• understanding shapes and other mathematical concepts

what you need
- Sandpaper
- Piece of wood, about 10" × 10" × ½"
- Damp cloth
- Pencil
- Ruler
- Hammer
- 81 finishing nails (¾" long)
- Rubber bands or yarn

what to do
1. Sand the piece of wood to remove any splinters, and then wipe with a damp cloth.
2. Draw an 8" × 8" square centered on the wood. Inside it, draw a grid of 1" squares.
3. Hammer in one nail where each line intersects another. Be sure the nail is hammered in securely but does not protrude through the back of the board.
4. Ask your child to experiment with making shapes by placing and stretching the rubber bands or yarn around different nails.

---

extra!

The following activities can provide your child with a head start and a deeper understanding of mathematical concepts:

- Draw and name shapes, such as rectangles, triangles, or hexagons, and ask your child to create the shapes on the board.

- Experiment to see how many different ways you and your child can mark off half of the board. Then try other fractional parts too.

- Measure the perimeter: create a square or rectangular shape and count the number of spaces between nails along each side.

- Measure the area: create a square or rectangular shape and count the number of boxes within this shape.

Out of This World

Have some off-the-wall fun with your child thinking of and using idioms.

Take any common idiom and compare its literal meaning to its commonly understood meaning.

ages: 6 years and up

skills:
- critical thinking
- language development

Suggest that your child illustrate the literal meaning of some of these expressions, for example:

- Off the wall
- Green with envy
- Up the creek without a paddle
- On thin ice
- Hot under the collar
- Way off base
- Over the hill

Ways to Weigh

Kids who are beginning to learn about weights and measurements and about addition and subtraction in school will enjoy these "weighty" games:

ages: 6 years and up

skills:
- measuring weight
- addition
- subtraction
- basic physics

How much together? Weigh your child and a heavy book separately. Add the numbers with your child. Then weigh your child holding the book to check your answer.

How much apart? So the kitten won't stand on the scale long enough for you to weigh it. Ask your child to hold it and weigh herself and the kitten. Then weigh your child by herself and subtract that weight from the total weight. The kitten weighs the difference!

How many pounds of pressure? To help your child see how much of his own weight he can lift, have him weigh himself.

Then have him weigh himself while pushing against a wall or sink. The difference between his whole weight and his weight while exerting pressure tells him how much of his own weight he can lift.

Meet Roy G. Biv

Roy G. Biv is a most colorful character whom your child will enjoy getting to know.

Roy doesn't really exist, but generations of kids have learned the names of the colors of the rainbow in order by memorizing his name, which spells out the first letter of all the colors—red, orange, yellow, green, blue, indigo, violet.

ages: 6 years and up

skills:
- critical thinking
- language development

See if you and your child can create another such aid for remembering a useful list. For example, "HOMES" might help her remember the Great Lakes: Huron, Ontario, Michigan, Erie, and Superior.

The Kid from W.O.R.D.

At this age, kids love to take in tidbits of information. Learning the meanings of anagrams will make any kid feel smarter. Here are some to get your started:

ages: 6 years and up
skills: • critical thinking • language development

SCUBA—Self-Contained Underwater Breathing Apparatus

NASA—National Aeronautics and Space Administration

SPCA—Society for the Prevention of Cruelty to Animals
Invite your child to make up a few of his own, such as:

WORD—Wide-Open Rollerblading Demonstration

KID—Kind in Deed

MOM—Most Outstanding Mathematician

Telling Time

"Wait a minute!" There's a phrase that kids are bound to hear a lot. But just how long is a minute? Make a game of comparing various time counters as you count off 60 seconds.

ages: 6 years and up
skills: • understanding time

Observe an egg timer, kitchen timer, and clock with a second hand for comparisons. Then, set up contests to see what can be accomplished in exactly one minute—putting on socks, running from the kitchen to an upstairs bedroom, drawing a self-portrait.

Magic Words

The more word games your child plays, the better! Here are some to get you started:

ages: 6 years and up

skills:
- vocabulary development
- spelling

Word series. Write a series of words, such as *ask, kite, eat, time, easel,* and *loop,* and ask your child to figure out how they're connected. (In this case, each word begins with the last letter of the previous word; any pattern you create will do.) Follow up by asking your child to provide a few more words for this list.

Word chains. Build words, one letter at a time. For instance, start with *a,* add *t* to make *at, h* to make *hat, c* to form *chat,* and finally *s* to make *chats.* See how long a word chain you can create.

---

extra!

For more of a challenge, try changing a *bat* into a *dog.* It's done one letter at a time, like this: *bat* to *bag,* to *bog,* to *dog.* Or change a *pig* into a *cat: pig, pit, pat, cat.*

Map Marking

Help your child learn geography and understand distance by marking a map with places you and your child have gone.

ages: 6 years and up

skills:
- understanding maps
- geography

If you're a world traveler, use a world map. If your trips tend to be domestic, stick to a United States or local map. Hang it on a wall and use pushpins or straight pins with colored tops to mark all the places your child has visited. Use different-colored pins to mark where in the world various friends and relatives live.

Map Puzzles

No doubt you have some old beat-up maps in the car that are crying out for a renewed use.

ages: 6 years and up

skills:
- understanding maps
- geography

Find a relatively unblemished section of a map, cover it with clear self-adhesive vinyl, and cut it into puzzle shapes for your child to put together.

Time Capsule

To help celebrate a birthday, the
New Year, or any other special
time, help your child create a time
capsule that he can open one to
ten years (or more!) hence.

ages: 6 years and up
skills:
• understanding time
• history

Find a tin container, and brainstorm with your child what items
might be interesting to look at in the future. Some suggestions:

- School or team photo
- Essay written or dictated by your child about what he expects the future to hold for him
- Marked copy of a television guide, highlighting his current favorite shows
- Today's newspaper
- Notes from his friends
- Menu from school lunch

Magnifying Glass

Using a store-bought magnifying glass is, in itself, a wonderfully exciting way to observe the world up close. It is even more fun for your child to make his own magnifier.

> **ages:** 6 years and up
>
> **skills:**
> - understanding of basic physics
> - light

what you need
- Sheet of plain white paper on which your child has drawn or written something
- Piece of clear glass, about 3" × 3"
- Crayon
- Water

what to do
1. Lay the paper under the glass.
2. Drawing very heavily, make a 1"-diameter circle with the wax crayon on the glass over a portion of the writing or drawing. Make sure there's a buildup of wax.
3. Put a droplet of water into the waxy circle. The portion of the writing or drawing under the water will appear larger. Like a magnifying glass, the water bends the light to enlarge the image.

Mirror Images

All you need here is a large mirror and a T-shirt with writing on it.

ages: 6 years and up
skills:
• critical thinking
• spatial reasoning

Children who are just learning to read are usually amazed the first time they look at themselves in a mirror when they're wearing a T-shirt with words on it. What happened to the letters? They're all backwards! Have your child write a message and hold it up to a mirror to see it reflected backwards.

Goo and Ooze

Here's a recipe for fun that proves things are not always as they appear.

ages: 6 years and up
prep time:
5 minutes
skills:
• basic physics
• tactile learning

what you need
- ½ cup cornstarch
- 2 Tbs. water
- Food coloring
- Small bowl
- Spoon

what to do

1. Mix the cornstarch, the water, and a drop or two of food coloring in the bowl, stirring them together with the spoon.
2. Let your child squeeze the mixture in his hands and see what happens. (The mixture looks like a solid but oozes like a liquid.)

Create a Flag

It's likely that your child sees at least one flag a day, but does she really stop to look at it and figure out what the colors and shapes mean? This activity will make her view flags with new appreciation.

ages: 6 years and up

skills:
• understanding symbols

what you need

• Flags to review, either real or pictures in a book or on an Internet site
• Plain white paper
• Crayons

what to do

1. Review a number of flags and point out what the various symbols mean, such as the stars on the U.S. flag representing the 50 current states and the stripes representing the 13 original colonies.
2. Suggest that your child think of symbols that could represent herself, her family, or her school.
3. Let her design and make her flag using paper and crayons.

Meet Book People

Encourage your child to write to a favorite contemporary author or illustrator.

ages: 6 years and up

skills:
- reading encouragement
- writing skills

You can write to any author or illustrator through his or her publisher, who will forward the letter, or, if you know where he or she lives, look up the name in the phone book or on the Internet, through a universal phone book or the publisher's Web site, which may allow you to e-mail the author directly. Children's bookstores and libraries often have author readings, which give your child a chance to meet the creators in person.

Lava Lamp

Lava lamps are back! What this one lacks in light, it makes up for in lovely lava.

ages: 6 years and up

prep time:
 10 minutes

skills:
- basic physics
- tactile learning

what you need
- Clear, clean jar with a tight-fitting lid
- Water

- Cooking oil
- Food coloring

what to do
1. Fill the jar with an equal mixture of water and oil. Notice that the oil and water never mix.
2. Add a few drops of food coloring. Notice that it mixes with the water, but not with the oil.
3. Screw on the lid and shake the jar.
4. Place the jar on the kitchen counter. Be patient as you wait and watch. Soon the colored water and oil will separate again.

Take a Poll

How many kids in the class prefer pepperoni pizza to plain slices? What are the five most popular baseball teams among first-graders? Which family members prefer vanilla ice cream to other flavors?

ages: 6 years and up
skills:
• critical thinking
• making comparisons
• math skills
• interviewing skills

Whatever interests your child is a good poll topic. Help her form questions to ask, choose people to interview, and tally the results.

Can You Break the Code?

Children love secrets. What could
be a better secret than a language
that others cannot read? Your
child will love making this code
himself!

ages: 6 years and up

prep time:
  15 minutes
skills:
  • critical thinking

what you need
• Pencil
• Paper

What to do
1. For an alphabet chart, make a 2-column chart of 26 lines
   on the paper. Write a letter in each square of the first column.
2. Write a symbol, a different letter, or a number in the second
   column, next to each letter of the alphabet.
3. Now think of a sentence to say in code.
4. Replace each letter in the sentence with the symbol under
   it. For example: If the letter *F* is represented by a #, *U* by
   *, and *N* by +, the word *FUN* becomes #*+.
5. Exchange notes with your child, each using the secret code.

---

extra!

For variety, make secret-code friendship bracelets. Write the alphabet on one strip of paper, cover it with transparent tape, and glue the ends together to make a bracelet. On an identical strip of paper, write the codes and form it into a bracelet, too. Make a mark on both to indicate where the two bracelets should line up. Make a second, identical set of strips for a friend. The bracelet sets can then be used to encode and decode your messages.

Personal Stationery

Instead of calling Grandma on the phone, why not write her a letter on a beautiful piece of homemade stationery?

ages: 6 years and up	
prep time: 15 minutes	
skills:	
• written expression	
• design concepts	

what you need
- Sheets of plain white paper
- Markers, paints, stickers, sparkles
- White glue or paste

what to do
1. Encourage your child to design some stationery with the recipient in mind. For example, if the letter is bound for a

gardener, decorate it with pictures of flowers. Think about spritzing a little perfume on it as well.

2. Let the child write a letter and mail it. He may want to design a special envelope as well.

Coin Rubbings

Coin rubbings are easy to do and exotic!

ages: 6 years and up
skills: • understanding money, dates, and history

Give your child a variety of coins, both domestic and foreign, a pencil or crayon, and a few sheets of paper. Place the coins on a table and lay the paper over them. With the side of a sharpened pencil tip or an unwrapped crayon, let your child make rubbings.

extra!

Coins lend themselves to a seemingly endless array of activities. Here are some:

- Discuss the values of different coins, letting your child arrange them in order of value.

- Ask your child to arrange the coins chronologically.

- Whose likeness is on the coin? What can your child find out about that person? What's shown on the flip side?

  Penny: Abraham Lincoln; flip side—Lincoln Memorial

  Nickel: Thomas Jefferson; flip side—Monticello, Jefferson's estate

  Dime: Franklin D. Roosevelt; flip side—torch and sprigs of oak and laurel

  Quarter: George Washington; flip side—eagle

  Half dollar: John F. Kennedy; flip side—presidential seal

  Silver dollar: Susan B. Anthony; flip side—eagle

- What do the different words and phrases on the coins mean? For example:

  What's the meaning of the word *liberty*, which is on all American coins?

  What about the Latin phrase *e pluribus unum* (out of many, one)?

Crossword Puzzles

Try teaching your child to do crossword puzzles. Make your own and work them out. It will be easier to acquire crossword-puzzle skills on a customized puzzle. Later, branch out to harder puzzles. All you need is paper and pencil.

ages: 6 years and up

prep time:
  15 minutes
skills:
  • critical thinking
  • word recognition

- Think of easy words your child knows and write them into a crossword-puzzle format. Then write the clues. Make a duplicate of your crossword format, filling in only the guiding numbers and blocked-out squares.
- Teach your child how to do this crossword puzzle.

Where in the World?

Making her own globe is a sure way for your child to develop an interest in geography. Let her do as much of this project as she is able.

ages: 6 years and up

prep time:
  1 hour, over 2 days
skills:
  • geography
  • research skills

what you need

- Papier-mâché or wallpaper wheat paste
- Basin
- Balloon
- Newspaper, torn into 1"-wide strips
- Map or globe (for reference)
- Paint
- Black marker

what to do

1. Prepare the papier-mâché mix or wallpaper paste in a basin according to the package directions. (See page 4 for directions for homemade papier-mâché.)
2. Blow up the balloon.
3. Dip a newspaper strip in papier-mâché mix or wallpaper paste and place it on the balloon. Continue doing this until the balloon is covered with about two layers of paper.
4. Let it dry for a day.
5. Referring to your globe or map, paint the balloon to depict oceans and continents.
6. Once the paint is dry, label the oceans and continents with black marker.

extra!

Older children may want to include more details on their globe. Suggest they paint or draw these specific sections of their map on plain paper first and then glue them to the dry papier-mâché globe.

PARENTS ALERT

Children under 6 should be supervised when using balloons, which are a choking hazard.

Organize a Library

Do you have trouble finding that special book in the bookcase? This activity will help solve that problem.

ages: 6 years and up	
prep time: 15 minutes	
skills:	
• categorizing	
• critical thinking	

what you need
- Your child's home library
- Adhesive file-folder labels or name tags
- Markers or crayons

what to do
1. Help your child sort his books according to categories (such as holiday books, number books, *ABC* books, chapter books, animal books).
2. Decide on an easy symbol with which to label each category and draw it in the middle of a sticker. For example, alphabet books might be designated by a capital *ABC*, animal books with a picture of a bear, and so on.

3. Place the illustrated label on the spine of a book in its category.
4. Continue until all books are labeled.
5. Group books by category on the bookshelf.
6. Instead of pictures, you may want to create a color code for each category, such as red for alphabet books or green for science books.

Make Up Math Problems

Kids can use calculators or paper and pencil to solve these problems. Have an encyclopedia handy for the figures, and encourage your child to make up some questions for you to solve, too.

ages: 7 years and up
skills:
• basic math operations
• research skills

• How many hours, days, or weeks is a million seconds? A million minutes?
• What's the difference between the average high and low temperatures in the city or town in which you live?
• How far is it from (any city) to (any city)? On a map with a scale of 1" for 10 miles, how many inches apart would they be?

Magic Math

Kids just learning multiplication and division may need an adult to help them challenge a bigger kid with magic math. (A player can substitute any number in Step 1; the result will always be 7.)

ages: 7 years and up
skills: • basic math operations • research skills

Here is what your child should say:

1. Think of a number—any number. (7)
2. Subtract 2 from that number. (7 − 2 = 5)
3. Multiply the remaining number by 3. (5 × 3 = 15)
4. Add 12. (15 + 12 = 27)
5. Divide the resulting number by 3. (27 ÷ 3 = 9)
6. Add 5. (9 + 5 = 14)
7. Take away your original number. (14 − 7 = 7)
8. Your sum is 7. How do I know? It's magic!

Turn on the Lights

A quick trip to the hardware store or the family junk drawer is all you need for this activity. Just present your child with the needed materials and then sit back and watch her imagination—and more—light up.

ages: 7 years and up
prep time: 15 minutes **skills:** • understanding   electricity

what you need
- 2 flashlight batteries
- Lengths of different types of wire, such as copper and steel, at least 1' each
- Flashlight bulb
- Tape
- Electrical switch (optional)
- Small motor that can be driven by batteries (optional)
- Scissors (to cut wire)
- Box, large enough to hold all of the above

what to do
1. Put all of the equipment in the box.
2. Issue the challenge to your child: Turn these ingredients into a working light.
3. Let her play.

Remember, even Ben Franklin had trouble with electricity in the beginning. If your child has difficulty, suggest that she think about electricity as a circle (circuit). Suggest that she line up the batteries, end to end, attaching the wire from one end of one battery to the opposite end of the other. When the light bulb is placed at the top nub of the wire and battery, she creates a circuit, making the power from the batteries travel through the wires to light the bulb. To keep the circuit going, she can tape all the items in place. Or, she can experiment with attaching the switch at any point along the circuit to make and break the connection. Or, instead of lighting a bulb, she can attach the motor to the circuit to make it go.

Enough Already!

Emergent readers are often stumped when they come across words like *enough* or *light,* which don't follow the phonics rules they're beginning to understand. Make a game out of finding words that have unusual spelling combinations, such as:

> **ages:** 7 years and up
>
> **skills:**
> * spelling
> * reading

PH for F: phone, elephant, photo, morph

GH for F: cough, tough, rough, laugh

KN for N: knot, know, knee, knife

Silent GH: light, night, right, fight, sigh, sight, height, eight

Your child also can make up silly sentences, using as many of these words as she can:

* The elephant didn't know my right phone number.
* I can laugh when I cough, but it's rough.

Graph Game

This quick and easy activity for two players can even be played in the car.

ages: 7 years and up
prep time: 5 minutes   **skills:**   • ordered pairs   • critical thinking

what you need
- Graph paper with as big a grid as you can find
- Pencil

what to do
1. On two identical sheets of graph paper, number the lines going down and across consecutively, beginning with "1" in the upper left-hand corner.
2. Each player gets a graph and puts a secret "X" at one of the intersecting points on the graph.
3. As one player holds the graph so only he can see it, the other selects a point on the graph and asks if the X is there. (The point is read by saying the numbers that represent where the X intersects on the horizontal and vertical lines. For example, Point 4-2 would be 4 across and 2 down.)
4. If the point guessed is correct, that player wins. If it's incorrect, the player crosses that point off so he does not ask the same location again.
5. It is now the second player's turn. She guesses a point. Once again, if it is not a "hit," she indicates it on her graph.
6. The game continues until one of the players guesses where the X is on the other player's graph.

the way it was

a look at games and crafts of the past

Back when a mouse was a rodent and not an essential part of a computer, kids occupied themselves by making entertaining and useful items from readily available materials. To ensure the right atmosphere, turn off the electricity while you make these crafts and toys from yesteryear. Then augment the experience by reading a book or watching a video set in the time that matches your project. The activities in this chapter are appropriate for children ages 4 and up.

Spool Trains

Here's an easy-to-make toy that demonstrates the popularity of used sewing spools.

ages: 4 years and up
prep time:
about 20 minutes
skills:
• eye-hand
coordination

what you need
- At least 6 pipe cleaners (1 pipe cleaner for the engine, 1 for the end car, and 2 for each middle car)
- 4 or more empty spools, 1 larger than all the others
- Paint or markers

what to do
1. Insert one pipe cleaner through the largest spool (the engine), one through another spool (the end car, or caboose), and two through each of the other spools.
2. Line up the spools on their sides (so they can roll), with the engine at one end.
3. Attach the engine to the second car by twisting the pipe-cleaner ends from the engine together with one pair of pipe-cleaner ends from the second car.
4. Attach the second car to the third by twisting together two sets of pipe-cleaner ends, and so on, until all the cars are connected. Finish with the caboose, with only one pipe cleaner. Be careful not to twist the pipe cleaners too tightly or the "wheels" won't turn.
5. Decorate the train with the paint or markers.

Scrimshaw

This activity shows what it was like in the days of whaling, when sailors made jewelry and ornaments from the teeth of whales. Let your child do as many of the steps as he is able.

ages: 5 years and up
prep time: 30 minutes
skills: • eye-hand coordination • learning about early whaling crafts

what you need
- Plaster of Paris
- Disposable plastic container for mixing
- Spoon
- Wax paper
- Nail
- Fine-tip markers

what to do
1. Mix the plaster in the plastic container according to the package directions.
2. Using the spoon, drop some dollops of plaster onto the wax paper.
3. Let the plaster dry thoroughly.
4. With the nail, scratch a picture or design in each dollop.
5. Using markers, darken the lines. Wipe away any excess ink to reveal the scrimshaw etching.

Totem Pole

Make your own totem pole to celebrate your family traditions.

ages: 5 years and up

prep time:
  30 minutes
skills:
  • learning about
    Native American
    traditions

what you need
- Scissors or craft knife
- Clean ½-gallon milk cartons, 1 for each family member
- White glue or paste
- Construction paper
- Markers, crayons, paints

what to do
1. Cut off the top and bottom of each milk carton.
2. Have your child glue construction paper around the outside of each carton.
3. Have each family member draw something relevant to the family on all four sides of a carton.
4. Show your child how to place the cartons end to end and push them a little bit inside each other to hold them in place.

Feather Pens and Cranberry Ink

Children are always curious about the way things used to be done. Here is a fun way to experiment with writing tools from colonial times. Making your own ink is an option; supervise your child if you choose to do so. (Cranberries stain, so a smock is a good idea for this project.)

ages: 6 years and up
prep time: about 20 minutes **skills:** • learning about Early American and European writing tools

what you need
- Craft knife or scissors
- Large feather
- ¼ cup cranberry juice in a small container
- Plain white paper

what to do
1. Cut a point into the bottom of the feather shaft.
2. Show your child how to dip the feather into the cranberry juice and write or draw on the paper.

---

extra!

To make your own ink, put 1 cup cranberries and ¼ cup water into a saucepan. Crush the berries with a wooden spoon and cook on the stove until they are soft. Use a wire strainer to strain the berry mixture into a small cup, and let cool.

Rag Doll

Just like children of long ago, yours will cherish a cuddly hand-made doll.

ages: 6 years and up
prep time: 1 hour skills: • manual dexterity • eye-hand coordination

what you need
• Pencil and paper
• 2 pieces of soft, easy-to-cut fabric, as wide and as tall as you plan to make the doll. Choose a skin-toned fabric, or a wild color or pattern for a more unique doll.
• Straight pins
• Scissors
• Sewing needles and embroidery thread or heavy thread
• Pillow stuffing or clean rags
• Permanent markers
• Yarn and buttons (optional)

what to do
1. Create a pattern by outlining the shape of the doll on paper. Avoid drawing pointy features by making feet and hands wide and rounded.
2. Smooth out the two pieces of fabric, right-sides together, on a flat surface. Lay the pattern on top of the fabric, and pin it to the two layers of fabric.
3. Cut out the fabric along the pattern outline. Remove the pattern and repin the pieces of fabric.
4. Thread the needle and knot the ends together.
5. Sew the two pieces of fabric together, making about four stitches to the inch inside the edge of the fabric. Leave a 2" section unsewn.

6. Turn the doll right-side out by pulling the fabric through this opening.
7. Stuff the doll and sew the opening closed.
8. Draw a face and hair with markers, or sew on buttons for facial features and yarn for hair.

Corn-Husk Doll

Native American children made dolls out of corn husks. Your child can, too!

ages: 6 years and up
prep time: 30 minutes, plus drying time **skills:** • fine motor skills

what you need
- Husks from 2–3 ears of corn, dried in the sun (to prevent mold)
- String or twist-ties
- Felt-tipped pen
- Magnets (optional)

what to do
1. To make a doll, fold two husks in half, from top to bottom.
2. Tie a string or twist a tie tightly, about an inch from the fold, to form the head.
3. Roll another husk lengthwise to form the arms, and slip this husk through the folded husk, just below the head.
4. Use another piece of string or twist-tie to tie off a waist, just below the arms.
5. To make a doll wearing a skirt, leave the husks below the waist loose to form the doll's skirt. For pants, divide the husks below the waist and tie off each leg at the ankle.
6. Draw a face on the doll with a felt-tipped pen.

---

extra!

Have your child glue a magnet to the back of the doll so it can be used as a refrigerator magnet.

Hand-Dipped Candles

Old candles can be transformed into beautiful new ones. A grown-up should melt the wax, but a 6-year-old can do the dipping himself.

ages: 6 years and up

prep time:
  30–45 minutes
skills:
  • traditional candle-making
  • basic physics

what you need
• Paraffin or candle stubs
• Electric skillet
• String for wicks, in 10" lengths
• 1-qt. container of cold water

what to do
1. Melt the wax in the electric skillet.
2. Hold one wick in the middle so the ends droop down.
3. Quickly dip both sides into the wax at once. Make sure to dip the wicks quickly or the wax won't adhere.
4. Next dip the two waxy wicks into cold water, and gently straighten the wicks.
5. Continue to alternate dipping into hot wax and cold water until the wax builds up on the wicks to the desired thickness.

6. Roll the candles on a cool, flat surface to straighten and flatten out any bumps.
7. Hang the candles by their wicks to dry overnight.

Tip To help remove the wax, fill the skillet with ice water and some salt before scrubbing.

 PARENTS ALERT

When it comes to melted paraffin or any other wax, adults must always supervise. Wax is extremely flammable and should never be melted in a saucepan (even in a double boiler) on the stove top.

Make Rock Candy

Here's an experiment that the kids will be sure to eat up. Your child can probably complete this project herself if you guide her through the directions and supervise the boiling of the water.

what you need
- Clean 16-oz. glass jar with a screw-on lid
- Hammer

ages: 6 years and up

prep time:
about 20 minutes, plus a few days' development time

skills:
- eye-hand coordination
- basic physics

- Nail
- Ruler
- 3 lengths of clean string, each about 5"
- Pencil or chopstick
- Paper clips, washed and dried
- 1 cup water in a saucepan
- 1¾ cups sugar
- Large spoon or whisk

what to do

1. Place the jar lid, open side down, on a protected, sturdy surface. With the hammer and nail, punch a row of three holes at ¾" intervals across the center of the lid.
2. Tie the 3 lengths of string to the pencil or chopstick at ¾" intervals.
3. Working from the top side of the lid, insert each string end through a hole in the lid. Then, tie a paper clip to each dangling end of the string.
4. Boil the water. Add the sugar to the saucepan. Stir, completely dissolving the sugar.
5. When the sugar water has cooled, pour it into the jar.
6. Screw on the jar lid so the paper clips dangle in the water without touching the bottom of the jar. If the strings are too long, roll the pencil or chopstick to shorten them.
7. Place the jar at room temperature where it will not be touched or moved. Leave it completely still for two to three days.
8. When crystals have formed, carefully unscrew the lid and lift out the crystal-encrusted paper clips. Some of the crystals may be as long as an inch. Simply enjoy their beauty or break the crystals off the paper clips and taste them.

PARENTS ALERT

Paper clips can be a choking hazard. Never let your child suck
the candy directly from the paper clips.

Skittles Game

This game has been around for a
few hundred years and has never
lost its appeal.

ages: 6 years and up
prep time:
 about 20 minutes
skills:
 • eye-hand
  coordination
 • traditional toy-
  making

what you need
• Craft knife or scissors
• 2 balsa-wood or cardboard
 strips, each 11" × 3"
• Black marker
• Wood or sturdy cardboard box, about 11" × 17" × 3"
• Tape, white glue, or paste
• Marbles

what to do
1. Cut three to four archways of varying widths in each wood
 or cardboard strip.
2. On both sides of each strip, label each archway according
 to a point system. For instance, the widest archway is worth
 1 point; the narrowest is worth 4 points.

3. Position the strips inside the box opposite one another, each about 2" from the ends the box. Tape or glue to secure.
4. Let kids take turns rolling a marble from one end (in front of the archway) to the other end (going through one of the archways) by tilting the box slightly. The goal is to score the most points for a set number of tries.

Corncob Pipes

Long ago, pipe smokers used these. Now kids can use them to blow bubbles. To give your child a real treat while recycling, make a pipe from a cob whose corn he has just enjoyed eating.

ages: 6 years and up
prep time: about 20 minutes, plus drying time
skills: • eye-hand coordination

what you need
- Corncob (cooked)
- Spoon or table knife
- Hammer
- 3" nail
- Piece of reed or a plastic straw
- Bubble mix (see page 5)

what to do
1. The middle of the corncob works best for making a pipe, so help your child cut or break off the ends, leaving a section of cob about 2 " long. He can finish the rest with your supervision.
2. With a spoon or table knife, scrape off any remaining corn kernels.

3. To make the pipe bowl, start at one end and scoop out the soft inside with the spoon or knife. Be sure not to break or cut too deeply into the sides of the bowl or to cut completely through to the other end.
4. With the hammer, gently tap the nail through the side of the cob near the bottom of the bowl, creating a hole large enough to fit a straw or reed. Leave the nail in place for now.
5. Let the cob dry overnight. Remove the nail and place the reed or plastic straw into the hole.
6. Pour a tablespoon or so of bubble mix into the pipe bowl and blow. Enjoy the cascade of bubbles.

Spool Dolls

Collect as many spools of different sizes as you can. Ask relatives and friends to save theirs, too. Craft stores also sell empty spools. Read these directions to your child if he cannot read them himself. He should be able to complete this project with just a little help from you.

ages: 6 years and up

prep time:
   about 20 minutes
skills:
   • eye-hand coordination

what you need
• Pipe cleaners, in 12" lengths (or shorter lengths, twisted together)
• 11 spools (at least 8 the same size)
• 4 wooden beads, about ½" in diameter
• Paint or markers

- Scissors
- Yarn
- Fabric scraps
- Paste or white glue

what to do

1. To make each leg and arm, have your child bend about 1" at one end of a pipe cleaner into the shape of a little hand or foot. Then, working with two of the eight same-size spools, insert the straight end of the pipe cleaner through a spool, a bead, and another spool to create a jointed arm or leg. Repeat three times to make the other arms and legs.
2. To make the torso, twist together three pipe cleaners and insert them through two spools.
3. To make the head, draw or paint a face on the remaining spool. To make the hair, cut about ten pieces of yarn into 4" lengths, hold them all together, and wrap one end of a pipe cleaner around the middle; insert the other end through the head spool.
4. Connect the limbs, body, and head by twisting the extending pieces of pipe cleaners together.
5. To make clothing for your doll, cut the fabric scraps into squares or rectangles to wrap around the torso, arms, and legs. Paste or glue on the clothing, being careful not to get glue on the beaded joints.
6. Pose the doll.

---

extra!

To make spool marionettes instead of posable dolls, use shoe-laces or yarn instead of pipe cleaners to attach all the parts, except the head, which should be attached to the torso using a pipe cleaner. Attach 12" lengths of clear plastic thread (such as fishing line) to the hands, 14" lengths to the feet, and 8" lengths to the torso of the puppet. Tie all loose ends of the thread together and direct the puppet to perform with a flick of the wrist.

---

close to nature

crafts and games from nature

The natural world provides all the materials your child needs for an advanced education. And it's fun, too!

In this section you'll discover new uses for nature's bounty, from ideas for making nature-based crafts to helping your child see and appreciate the world around her.

Water Painting

There's lots of fun (and no mess) when your child creates works of art with water. All you need is a brush, a bucket of water, and a smooth, dark surface.

ages: 12 months and up
skills: • manual dexterity

Outdoors in good weather, the sidewalk makes a great canvas. Have your child use a house painter's brush with a pail of water to create lines, circles, and other shapes. Talk about how the water makes marks and how the sun makes the marks go away. The sunnier the day, the more quickly your child's work will evaporate, a process that will intrigue her. Discuss wetness and dryness with her. Talk about how other things dry in the sun, such as laundry, and how rain makes things wet and how the sun dries everything again. With older children, make a game of trying to finish painting a large scene before it evaporates.

When water-painting indoors, choose absorbent construction paper for a canvas. Offer your child a small paintbrush to use on paper. She may also enjoy making water handprints or footprints. Simply have her put a wet hand or foot squarely on a piece of absorbent, dark paper. Join her in this activity and compare your handprints and footprints.

Puddle Power

A puddle is an entire universe to a toddler. Head out after a rain and when you happen upon a puddle, encourage your child to:

ages: 12 months and up
skills: • basic physics

Find out how deep it is. Dip a stick into the center to test its depth.

Jump in. If it's not too deep and he's wearing the right footwear, encourage him to jump through it.

Observe the reflections. Match what's above to what's reflected.

Drop in a pebble. Talk about the rippling effect.

Set sail. Place a leaf or other object that's likely to float in the puddle and see what happens.

Leaf Bouquet

Newly fallen leaves offer wonderful experiences with color, texture, and shapes.

Lead your child on a leaf hunt, collecting handfuls. At home, tie them with a ribbon for a beautiful bouquet.

ages: 18 months and up
skills: • categorizing

extra!

The number of activites that your child can do with leaves is inexhaustible. Here are just a few ideas:

• Help your child paste a number of different kinds of leaves onto paper to make a wall hanging.

• Wash some leaves in soapy water and rinse. Then let your child take them into the bath to watch them float amid the bubbles.

• Let him use leaves instead of paintbrushes for water painting (see page 231).

Stick Drawings

Show your child what a stick can do in the dirt, in the sand, or even in a puddle.

18 months and up
skills: • eye-hand coordination

Draw a shape and let her copy it. Draw a circle and jump into it. Draw a smiley face and ask her to make her own smile. You get the idea.

---

extra!

There's really no end to what your child can do with sticks. For older kids, try these ideas:

- Stick letters. Simply line up a number of twigs to form alphabet letters, explaining that, with sticks, it's perfectly okay to make square O's and to square off any rounded parts of letters.

- Stick art. Make a game of taking turns adding sticks to enlarge a design, such as a house, a stick-figure person, or anything else that suits your child's imagination

- Tic-tac-toe. Make a grid of sticks and use pebbles and bark for markers.

Catch Shadows

Point out your and your child's shadows.

ages: 2 years and up
skills: • gross motor skills

Play a game of tag, touching shadows only. Show your child how to observe his shadow in front of him. Have him turn around and observe his shadow from behind. If he turns left, where is his shadow? What happens to it when he scrunches himself into a ball? Can he find shadows of trees, cars, and park benches, too? Go on a shadow search!

What Does it Feel Like?

Noticing different textures adds a whole new element to your child's world.

ages: 2 years and up
skills: • sensory skills • language development

Guide your child's hand across the lawn. What does the grass feel like? What does the bark of a tree feel like? How is it different from grass? From sand? From water in a stream? How is a stone similar to the metal gate around the playground? Help your child find the words to describe *soft, rough, cold, hard,* and other attributes.

Smell the Flowers

Look for fragrant flowers and
show your child how to sniff.

If a flower has fallen from its stem,
or if you've got a ready-made bouquet from which you don't mind
losing one flower, help your child
take it apart so he can examine it thoroughly.

ages: 2 years and up	
skills:	
• sensory skills	
• language development	

Build a Boat

The next time you happen upon a
stream, quiet lake, or even a large
puddle, help your child assemble
a boat from twigs, leaves, pinecones, and other natural materials.

ages: 2 years and up	
skills:	
• visual tracking	
• understanding the properties of water and other materials	

If your vantage point is near
running water, follow your boat's
path alongside the stream as long as possible. If you're near
a bridge, place your little boat upstream and watch it from
your perch as it meanders downstream, under the bridge.

The Itsy Bitsy Spider

This activity helps your child see the beauty, simplicity, and intricacy of nature. You'll need the help of a web-spinning spider to get started.

ages: 3 years and up
prep time: 5 minutes
skills: • appreciation of nature

what you need
- Spiderweb
- Hair spray
- Construction paper
- Small plastic spider and/or glitter (optional)

what to do
1. Find an abandoned web, spray it with the hair spray, and then delicately press the paper to it. The hair spray acts like glue, and the spiderweb will stick to the paper.
2. Have your child examine the spiderweb up close.
3. Decorate it with a pretend spider or glitter for an interesting look.

Ice Sculpting

Building with blocks of ice is a fun warm-weather activity. Kids will especially enjoy donning mittens while wearing a bathing suit! All you need are blocks of ice and, for neatness if you're playing indoors, a plastic tablecloth.

ages: 3 years and up
skills: • eye-hand   coordination

what to do

1. Make a few batches of ice cubes. Also make larger blocks by filling pint- and quart-size milk cartons with water and freezing them.
2. Place the ice cubes on a cookie sheet or other flat surface where they won't adhere to one another.
3. Remove the larger ice blocks from their molds and place them on a level work surface.
4. Let your child build ice structures. Show him how sprinkling some salt on the cubes and blocks helps them adhere to one another.

At the beginning, the challenge will be keeping the slippery blocks from sliding off one another. As the activity continues, the melting ice blocks will meld into one another, creating a lovely, albeit temporary, ice structure. This is a great activity to keep kids amused during outdoor parties.

Wind Watching

Which way is the wind blowing? How strong is it? What can it do? Help your child observe and understand wind by placing a variety of windcatchers outside her window. Good choices include:

ages: 3 years and up

skills:
- appreciation of nature
- observation
- comparing

- Wind socks
- Weather vanes
- Pinwheels
- Balloons tied with string
- Wind chimes

On walks, point out signs of the wind's movement—on large flags in public places, on laundry lines, on falling leaves.

Talk with your child about how the wind affects each object. Show her that she can make wind, too, by demonstrating blowing on a tissue or blowing out a birthday candle.

Read *The Three Little Pigs* together and talk about how the different houses withstand (or don't) the wolf's huffing and puffing.

 PARENTS ALERT

Ensure that your child does not have access to any broken balloon pieces because they are a choking hazard.

You Need a Haircut

Help your child with these steps. He will love to watch this little guy's hair grow.

ages: 3 years and up

prep time:
   10 minutes

skills:
   • seed growth
   • measuring
   • graphs

what you need
- Markers
- Undecorated polystyrene cup
- Dirt or potting soil, enough to fill cup
- 1 Tbs. grass seed
- Water

what to do
1. Draw a face on the outside of the cup, positioned so that the forehead is right below the top of the cup. Do not draw hair.
2. Fill the cup with dirt or potting soil.
3. Place the grass seed on top of the dirt. Add water.
4. Put in a sunny place and wait. Soon the grass will grow and it will appear that the drawn figure is growing green hair.
5. When the "hair" gets long enough, let your child give it a trim.

extra!

With older children you may also want to get a ruler, and measure the growth of the "hair" each day. Make a bar graph showing the growth over a period of a few weeks.

Underwater Exploring

There is a whole other world underwater. Your child will be in on it firsthand with this underwater mask.

ages: 3 years and up	
prep time: 10 minutes	
skills:	
• manual dexterity	
• observation skills	

what you need

- Scissors
- ½-gallon milk carton, empty and clean
- Heavy-duty 1-gallon clear plastic food-storage bag
- Packing tape

what to do

1. Cut off the top and bottom of the milk carton.
2. Cut off the open end of the food-storage bag, creating a bag about 6" deep.
3. Place the milk carton in the bag, stretching the plastic tautly over one open side. Wrap the remaining part of the bag closely around the milk carton and tape to secure.
4. Submerge the plastic-covered bottom of the carton in a pond, puddle, or even a bucket of water or bathtub so your child can look at the world "under the sea."

Study Your Shadow

Children have a special friend—their shadow. At a certain time in their development they are acutely aware of it, and every so often they stop to see if it is still with them. Why not use this innate curiosity to help them learn even more about it?

ages: 3 years and up
prep time: 5 minutes
skills:
• measuring
• understanding the position of the sun

what you need
- Sunny area of pavement
- Chalk
- Tape measure or ruler (for older children)

what to do
1. Beginning in the morning, go out at different times of the day and trace the outline of your child's shadow with chalk. Be sure she is standing in the same place and facing in the same direction each time.
2. Each time you do this play a game called "I Spy the Sun," and have your child point to the direction of the sun, without looking at it directly. Discuss where the sun is in the sky and how long your child's shadow is at that moment.
3. Before each new shadow tracing, ask your child to guess if her shadow will be longer or shorter or pointed in a different direction than at the previous sighting.

---

extra!

For older kids, point out that as the earth moves around the sun, the position of the sun in the sky changes and that, as it does, their shadows get bigger or smaller. Have them use a tape measure or ruler to measure the length of their shadows from heel to head at various times of day. Let them graph their observations.

Regrow Dinner Greens

Use the top of a carrot or an avocado pit to give your child an almost instant garden.

ages: 3 years and up
prep time: 5 minutes, plus growing time **skills:** • observation

what you need
- Toothpicks
- Carrot top, with 1"–2" of root, or clean avocado pit
- Tall, clear glass or jar, about 12-oz. capacity
- Water
- 8" flowerpot with potting soil

what to do
1. Stick three or four toothpicks horizontally around the carrot top or avocado pit, so they radiate like the spokes of a wheel.
2. Fill the glass or jar two-thirds to three-quarters full with room-temperature water.

3. Insert the carrot top or avocado pit into the glass or jar so that the toothpicks rest on the rim.
4. Place the glass or jar in a cool spot that gets some light, but not in direct sunlight.
5. After a few days' time, the carrot top will sprout additional leaves and roots. The avocado pit will burst open, sprouting a treelike shoot, and will spread roots into the water.
6. After either plant has grown a few inches, transfer it to the pot with potting soil and watch what happens. (The carrot may or may not continue to sprout new leaves and roots. The avocado, most likely, will grow into an enormous plant. Cut it back occasionally to keep it healthy and transfer it to larger pots as it grows.)

Potpourri Sachet

Nature sure can smell great! Save and savor the aroma of blossoms with these easy-to-make potpourri sachets. Your local florist is likely to donate fallen petals to the cause if you don't have your own garden nearby. Younger children

ages: 3 years and up	
prep time: 5 minutes	
skills:	
• sensory observation	

can help collect the ingredients; older kids can also do the sewing. Sachet adds a lovely scent to socks, underwear, or T-shirts when placed in a dresser drawer. The pouches also make great gifts.

what you need
- Variety of dried petals (roses are particularly aromatic) or fresh pine needles

- 2 squares of lightweight fabric, about 6" × 6" each
- Thread and needle
- Ribbon (optional)

what to do

1. Collect a variety of petals. Experiment to see which fragrances work well together. For instance, your child could make an entire potpourri from one type of petal or from pine needles, or might like to mix several varieties.
2. Place one fabric square on top of the other, right-sides out, and sew together along three edges with a straight stitch.
3. Place the dried petals or fresh pine needles inside the fabric pouch, and sew up the remaining edge.
4. Sew on a pretty ribbon, if desired.

---

extra!

To quick-dry petals, spread them on a cookie sheet and bake them for about 5 minutes at 250°F.

Paint with Vegetables

Instead of expensive store-bought rubber stamps, try these easy-to-make alternatives. Try making wrapping paper or stationery using veggie stamps for a nice homemade touch.

ages: 4 years and up
prep time: 15 minutes
skills: • printmaking   • manual dexterity   • letter and shape recognition

what you need
- Vegetables or fruits such as potatoes, apples, and other solid, relatively dry varieties
- Markers
- Paring knife or sturdy plastic knife
- Finger-paints and paper plates, or ink pads
- Paper

what to do
1. Cut each vegetable in half.
2. Have your child outline shapes, such as stars or letters, onto each item. Cut away the surface around the design with a kitchen knife. If your child is old enough, let him cut with a plastic knife.
3. Show your child how to dip the raised design in paint poured onto paper plates or how to press the design lightly on an ink pad. Then print the design on paper.

Leaf Creatures

Show your child how to appreciate the differences in leaves all year round.

ages: 4 years and up
prep time: 5 minutes, plus drying time **skills:** • basic botany • appreciation of nature

Like people, leaves come in all shapes, sizes, and colors. They also form the basis for some amazing artwork that kids will never tire of creating. Simply collect a few leaves, paste them to construction paper, hand out crayons, and prepare for some really fun results. Ask you child to name or identify his creatures.

Blue Celery

With this experiment, prove that plants "drink."

ages: 4 years and up
prep time: 5 minutes, plus waiting time **skills:** • basic botany • understanding how plants absorb water

what you need
• Stalk of celery
• Tall glass filled with water
• Blue food coloring

what to do

1. Cut off the end of the stalk of celery.
2. Take the glass of water and add enough food coloring to turn the water deep blue.
3. Place the celery in the colored water. After a few hours, you will notice that blue streaks are appearing along the sides of the celery and that the leaves are turning blue. This proves that the celery drank the water and shows where the water goes in the plant.

Bird Feeder and Birdbath

Help birds set up house in your yard!

ages: 4 years and up
prep time: 10 minutes
skills: • fine motor skills • observation

To make a bird feeder, spread a pinecone with plain suet (available in a grocery) or suet mixed with flour. Roll it in some bird-seed and hang it from a tree by a wire or twine. Observe the birds feasting. (Don't substitute peanut butter for suet; it can cause birds' beaks to seal shut.)

For a birdbath, fill a plastic plant saucer or an overturned Frisbee with warm water. Place it on a picnic table or other perch where birds, but not other critters, can reach it easily. Put a stone in the center to keep it from blowing away.

Picture This!

Create something beautiful from a collection of items found around the yard.

ages: 4 years and up	
prep time: 30 minutes **skills:** • sorting • appreciation of nature	

what you need
- Photo or other picture to frame
- Scissors and craft knife
- Cardboard
- Items found in nature such as pebbles, twigs, or shells
- White glue or paste
- Tape

what to do
1. Have your child decide what shape to make his picture frame. Help him cut the cardboard to the shape desired. Make the frame opening about ½" smaller all around than the size of the photo.
2. Let your child arrange the natural items on the frame.
3. Working on one side at a time, have him remove the items, spread the white glue or paste generously on the cardboard, and then replace the items in the glue or paste. Let the glue or paste dry.
4. Center the picture behind the frame and tape it in place.

Solar Power

Kids already know that the sun is
hot. These experiments give them
some ideas on how to harness
that heat—and how to reduce its
effects, too.

ages: 4 years and up
skills:
• understanding solar power
• understanding how dark colors absorb the sun and light colors reflect it

Experiment with light and dark.
Which attracts heat—light or dark?
Which repels heat? This experi-
ment will let you know: Have your child place two pieces of
paper or cloth—one black and one white—on a table in bright
sunlight. (Weight them with a rock.) She can check in about
an hour and see which one is hotter. Explain that dark colors
attract heat and light ones repel heat. Ask your child what
color clothing might be better to wear on a hot, sunny day and
what might be better on a winter's day.

Make sun tea. Fill a large covered jar, at least 32 ounces, with
water and have your child place two tea bags inside. Place the
covered jar in a sunny spot. Wait a few hours and enjoy a
glass of sun-brewed tea. Add ice, some lemon juice, and a bit
of sugar for some homemade iced tea.

Make sun prints. For this project, you'll need one black and
one white sheet of construction paper. Ask your child to cut
out a design on the black paper and place it on top of the
white paper. Place both papers in the sun for an hour or more.
(Use a rock to weigh the papers down.) The cutout design will
create a negative image on the white paper.

Make a solar oven. Help your child wrap heavy-duty alumi-num foil around two pieces of cardboard, each about 12" square. Make sure the shiny side of the foil is facing out. Aim one piece of foil-covered board at the sun and place the other, about 12" away, facing the first piece. Hold the two foil-covered boards in place with stones. Your child can place a potato or even a piece of bread between the two boards. The bread will toast in just a few minutes. The potato will bake in about an hour.

 PARENTS ALERT

Don't leave this solar oven unattended in the sun. It could har-ness enough heat to start a fire.

Make Tracks

Have you ever seen an animal footprint out in the yard and won-dered what left its tracks behind? Why not take that print into the house and try to identify it! Here's how.

ages: 4 years and up

prep time:
  30 minutes
skills:
  • critical thinking
  • research skills

what you need

- 1 cup plaster of Paris
- ⅔ cup water
- Container and spoon for mixing

what to do

1. Find a footprint or let your child make one himself in the mud. Perhaps the family pet can lend a paw.
2. Let your child mix the plaster and water in the container and then pour the mixture into the print.
3. Wait until it is dry and lift out the plaster.

---

extra!

Here are a couple of "next steps" you and your child might take:

- If the print is that of an animal or a bird, consult a book to learn more about the critter.

- While your child is away, make a print in the dirt using a family member's shoe. Invite your child to examine the print and to try to identify whose shoe made it.

Multi-Colored Carnations

Let your child create a two-colored carnation—and see again how plants absorb water.

ages: 4 years and up
prep time: 5 minutes, plus waiting time
skills:
• basic botany
• understanding how plants absorb water

what you need
- 2 tall glasses
- Water
- 2 colors of food coloring
- Utility knife
- White carnation

what to do
1. Fill each glass with water and mix a different food coloring into each. Place the glasses side by side.
2. Slice the stem of the carnation along the middle, being sure to leave the blossom securely attached, and place half the stem in one glass and the other half in the other glass.
3. Let stand overnight. The next day you'll see that the carnation has absorbed the two colors of the water.

★ Also see "Blue Celery" on page 247.

Mary, Mary, How Does Your Garden Grow?

Whether you live in the country, where there is lots of backyard space to plant, or in the city, where a sunny windowsill is all that's available, your child can learn numerous skills by planting and tending her own vegetable garden. As an extra bonus, she can eat the results! When choosing seeds, find the ones that will grow best in your environment.

ages: 4 years and up
prep time: ½ hour over   a number of days   **skills:**   • measuring   • planting   • observing the   growing process

what you need
- Packets of seeds
- Small patch of dirt, suitable for planting (for outdoor gardeners)
- Flower pots and potting soil (for indoor gardeners)
- Digging tools
- Ruler

what to do
1. Read the seed packets to your child, noting the kind of soil needed, how deep and how far apart to plant the seeds, and the light and watering requirements.
2. Let your child prepare the soil and make the furrows. Help her use the ruler to measure depth and spacing.

3. Let her plant the seeds and cover them with soil and water as directed on the packets.
4. Make daily or every-other-day observations and have your child describe what she observes.

---

extra!

If your child finds she enjoys gardening, try guiding her through these activities:

- Using the same kinds of seeds, experiment to see what happens if you plant them in less or more sun than recommended.

- Plant the ingredients for a specific recipe, such as tomatoes, basil, and oregano for making tomato sauce, or a number of greens for making a salad.

Cloud Watching

Nothing beats a warm afternoon spent lying on a soft surface watching the clouds drift by. It's a great activity to share with your child, bringing back all sorts of wonderful childhood memories of your own.

ages: 4 years and up

skills:
- imagination
- language development

With your child, pick out a cloud and decide what it looks like. Using a library book as your guide, introduce your child to the words *cirrus* (high-altitude wispy clouds) and *cumulus* (puffy, low-altitude clouds), and try to identify each kind in the sky.

Mini Log Cabin

Using much of the same technology as the pioneers used—though on a far smaller scale—your child can build a log cabin that would make any woodsman proud.

ages: 4 years and up
prep time: 20 minutes
skills: • eye-hand coordination • building

Begin with a few dozen twigs. Mix some mud and grass for mortar. Then demonstrate cross-stacking the twigs and layering in the mortar to hold the "logs" together. Let your child complete the building you've started and build others of her own design.

Rub a Tree

All your child needs for this truly satisfying experience is a large piece of paper, a crayon, and a tree.

ages: 5 years and up
skills: • eye-hand coordination

Show him how to use the side of an unwrapped crayon to capture the intricate design of the nooks and crannies of the bark on the paper. He can either hold the paper in place on the trunk with one hand as he rubs with the crayon with the other, or he can use masking tape to attach the paper to the tree while he works.

Suggest that your child use the same method to reveal the detailed designs on bricks and sidewalks. Older children who are studying local lore might want to make rubbings of the headstones of prominent citizens in the town's history.

Catch Critters

Many adults have fond memories of catching fireflies in a jar. Pass the tradition down to your child, and create some others.

ages: 5 years and up
skills: • understanding insects

Firefly jar. A 32-oz. plastic or glass jar with a lid can make a nice temporary home for a firefly.

Line the bottom with grass and leaves. Punch holes in the lid. Show your child how to catch a bug gently in the cup of his hands and transfer it to the jar. Give your child time to examine the insect as it lights up. Be sure to free the firefly close to where you caught it.

Ant home. Place a few sweet crumbs on a piece of cardboard and lay it next to an anthill. It won't be long until a small army marches across the board. Have a magnifying glass handy to get a close-up look at the activity; just be sure to conduct your viewing in the shade. (Beaming the sunlight directly onto an ant through a magnifier will injure or kill the ant.)

Butterfly net. An old mesh onion bag, a ring made by bending wire, and a wooden or cardboard pole (such as a paper-towel tube) are the makings of a butterfly net. Weave the wire through the openings of the onion-bag mesh, and attach it with heavy-duty tape to the handle. Demonstrate how to carefully lower the net over a butterfly. Give your child a chance to examine its beautiful wing design before gently releasing it.

---

extra!

If your child wants to wear a number of butterflies, suggest that she don a brightly colored, flowery shirt and stand in any butterfly habitat, such as a garden. It's very likely that any nearby butterfly will temporarily mistake your child for a bouquet and alight on her shoulder.

Stick Room Sign

Here's a fun and easy way for your child to review writing her name—and it makes a woodsy door decoration, too.

ages: 5 years and up
prep time: 15 minutes **skills:** • letter formation

what you need
• White glue or paste
• Sturdy piece of cardboard
• Twigs
• Leaves, shells, or other natural finds
• Dowel or blunted pencil
• Twine

what to do
1. Have your child write the letters of her name with glue or paste on the cardboard.
2. Have her cover the glue or paste with twigs to form three-dimensional letters.
3. Use the glue or paste to attach decorations of leaves, shells, or other natural finds. Let the glue or paste dry.
4. Punch two holes along the top of the sign, string some twine through the holes, and hang the natural nameplate on her bedroom door.

Build a Terrarium

An indoor garden that requires no maintenance is a perfect first garden for any child. Once you've cut the bottles, your child should be able to create the terrarium herself.

ages: 5 years and up	
prep time: 30 minutes	
skills:	
• eye-hand coordination	
• basic gardening	

what you need
- 2-liter soda bottle, with screw-on top
- Craft knife
- Pebbles, enough to line the bottom of the bottle
- Soil
- Two attractive rocks
- Small, sturdy indoor plants (such as a philodendron)
- Clear packing tape

what to do
1. Remove the label from the bottle and cut the bottle in half around the middle.
2. Layer the bottom part of the bottle with pebbles to allow drainage and air circulation.
3. Add about 3" of soil on top of the rocks.
4. For decoration, put two rocks on top of the soil.
5. Plant a few small indoor plants in the soil. Water them well.
6. Reattach the top of the bottle with clear packing tape. Tighten the bottle cap securely.
7. Place the terrarium in an area with indirect light. It will not need to be watered frequently, but if it begins to dry out, unscrew the cap and water the plants again, and then recap it tightly.

Grow Icicles

Thanks to improved insulation, icicles hanging from eaves are not nearly as common a sight as they once were.

ages: 5 years and up
prep time:
10 minutes, plus waiting time
skills:
• basic physics
• understanding how cold affects water

Bring back the magic by poking a tiny hole in the bottom of a plastic container, such as a small beach bucket or even a milk carton. Hang the container from a tree limb or porch roof, in an area that no one is likely to walk under. Fill the container with water and set it out on a frigid night. The next morning, your child will be treated to a lovely icicle.

Seed Art

Instead of crayons or markers, use different-colored seeds to paint a picture. Your child can choose sunflower, pumpkin, or other edible seeds or smaller flower seeds. (If he uses flower seeds, be sure that they are a nontoxic variety.)

ages: 5 years and up
prep time:
30 minutes
skills:
• critical thinking
• planning
• color categorizing

To start his seed-art project, suggest that your child draw the outline of a design or scene on a piece of paper. Then have him separate the seeds according to color. Have him spread some white glue on one section of the drawing at a time and sprinkle on the seeds needed for that area. Then move on to the next section.

He can make a decorative wall hanging by gluing seeds to cardboard or felt instead of paper. Add yarn and outdoor finds such as pinecones.

Waterfall

There is no better fun than water play. This silly game allows your child to explore the properties of water and to test his ability to predict what will happen. To avoid spills, it's best to do this one outdoors.

ages: 5 years and up
prep time: 15 minutes
skills: • prediction

what you need
- 4 or more clean metal juice cans, 32-oz. size, empty, with one end removed
- Nail
- Hammer
- Ladder or step stool
- Water

what to do

1. On all but one can, puncture a hole in the side near the bottom, using the nail and hammer.
2. Help your child put the cans on consecutive steps of the ladder or step stool; the can with no hole sits on the ground. Align the cans one above the other, with the holes facing outward. Let him fill the top can with water and watch as it drips from can to can.
3. Ask him to predict how long it will take for the water to completely fill the bottom can.

Twig Vase

Here's an idea from home decorators that your child will love. You might have her make a few to give you as gifts. Once you explain the process to your child, she'll be able to do this alone.

ages: 5 years and up

prep time:
  30 minutes
skills:
  • manual dexterity

what you need

- Empty coffee can or jar
- White glue or paste
- Large handful of twigs, each about 6" long
- Twine or ribbon

what to do

1. Cover a 2"- to 3"-wide section of the outside of the can or jar from top to bottom with glue or paste.

2. Carefully press the twigs into the glue or paste. Repeat for each section, until the entire can or jar is covered.
3. Wrap a piece of twine or ribbon around the finished vase for some extra decoration as well as extra pressure to hold the twigs in place.

Walnut-Shell Critters

After eating a batch of delicious walnuts, hold on to those shells.

ages: 5 years and up
prep time: 15 minutes
skills:
• manual dexterity
• creativity

what you need
- Nutcracker or paring knife
- Walnuts
- Paint and paintbrushes (optional)
- White glue or paste
- Pom-poms, small craft eyes, scraps of cloth or ribbon, pipe cleaners
- Magnet (optional)

what to do
1. Open a walnut shell, keeping the shell halves intact.
2. Have your child look in a book or the backyard and observe the attributes of various bugs.
3. Let her paint the shells (optional).
4. Have her glue or paste pom-poms, craft eyes, bits of cloth

or ribbon, and pipe cleaners to the shell to replicate the bug's legs, antenna, and facial features.
5. Turn the critter into a refrigerator magnet by gluing a magnet to the underside.

Paper-Towel Garden

With just a few things, your child can make a window garden—a perfect way to observe plant growth. Explain this process to your child; he can do it by himself.

| ages: 5 years and up |
| prep time:
 20 minutes
skills:
 • research skills
 • observation |

what you need
- Paper towel
- Sealable plastic sandwich bag
- Stapler
- Flower or grass seeds
- 1 Tbs. water
- Flowerpot and potting soil (optional)

what to do
1. Fold a paper towel in half and in half again (quarter it).
2. Place the folded towel flat in a plastic sandwich bag.
3. Staple in a line across the middle of the bag, through the towel, allowing ½" between staples.
4. Insert the seeds into the bag, placing them between the towel and the plastic, and resting them on the staples.

5. Add about a tablespoon of water and seal the bag.
6. Hang the bag in indirect sunlight and watch the seeds grow.
7. After 2–3 days, remove and plant in a flowerpot and potting soil or discard.

Seashell Wind Chime

No child can resist collecting beautiful shells at the beach. Add a piece of driftwood and some fishing line or curling ribbon, and you've got the makings for a beautiful wind chime.

ages: 5 years and up

prep time:
  20 minutes
skills:
  • eye-hand
    coordination
  • basic gardening

Suggest that your child collect about six shells that have tiny holes bored by nature or that have shapes around which she can securely tie fishing line or ribbon. Have her tie 10" of line or ribbon to each one and then attach the other end to a piece of driftwood. Use additional line or ribbon to hang the driftwood from a branch or porch roof. The sounds made as the shells clack against each other in the breeze are soothing.

For the Birds

It is always fun to watch the birds.

Next time, have your child take a piece of paper with him and look closely. What do the beak and feet look like? What colors and patterns are on the wings? What does the bird eat? Where is its nest? Have your child draw and color all he can observe about the bird.

ages: 6 years and up
prep time: 1 hour, over 2 days
skills: • observation

---

extra!

Indoors, consider other media in which to render a bird: out of clay, with pipe cleaners covered with tissue paper, or with a sponge or vegetable stamp. (See pages 52 and 246.) Also try photographing the bird in a series of positions and locations or writing a story about it.

Corn-Husk Wreath

Instead of throwing out your corn
husks in the summer, lay them out
in the sun to dry so they won't get
moldy, and then make a pretty
wreath with them. Read the directions with your child as she is
ready to do each step.

ages: 6 years and up	
prep time: 30 minutes	
skills:	
• fine motor skills	

what you need
- Pliers
- Wire coat hanger
- Husks from about 20 ears of corn, dried out
- Decorative ribbon or small ears of Indian corn and thin wire

what to do
1. Use pliers to bend the triangular part of the wire coat
   hanger into a circle, leaving the hook so you can hang the
   finished wreath.
2. Fold a corn husk in half lengthwise and then tie in a tight
   knot around the wire. (If you find the husks are too brittle,
   try soaking them in lukewarm water for 15 minutes. You
   don't need to redry them before folding and knotting.)
3. Repeat, folding and tying more husks onto the wire. Push
   the husks tightly together. Continue circling the wire with
   knotted husks until no wire remains visible. Arrange the
   knots to face inside or outside the wreath, or in any combination you like.
4. Tie ribbon or wire a bunch of Indian corn to the top of the
   wreath, right below the hook.
5. Hang the wreath on the front door or on a window, either
   indoors or out.

Weave a Flower Crown

Dandelions are never considered weeds by kids in the know. Instead, they're the makings of a lovely flower crown.

ages: 6 years and up
prep time: 30 minutes **skills:** • eye-hand   coordination

After your child collects a dozen or more dandelions or other blossoms with stems, you can demonstrate the fine art of chaining them together to form a flower crown.

Simply tie a loop with one stem, close to the bud. Place another stem through the loop, and then make a second loop with *that* stem. Keep going until the garland is long enough to circle into a crown.

Save a Nest

The home the birds left behind can be recycled into a learning tool for your child.

ages: 6 years and up
skills: • observation

In autumn, after the birds have flown to their winter homes, scour the neighborhood park or your own backyard for abandoned nests. Wearing gloves, re-move the nest, bring it home, and take a good look. Have your child observe the nest's materials, weaving pattern, and other characteristics. Look in a book to find out what species built it and how many eggs the nest likely held.

Make a Wall Hanging

While taking a nature walk, why not bring along a bag and collect a few special objects to incorporate into a weaving? Twigs, feathers, and flowers will give a wall hanging a special look. Read the directions with your child as she's ready to do each step.

ages: 6 years and up	
prep time: 30 minutes	
skills: • eye-hand coordination	

what you need
- Scissors
- Yarn or twine, about 15 yards, assorted colors
- 2 fairly straight small branches, each about 14" long
- Masking tape
- Natural items such as twigs, feathers, seedpods, and flowers

what to do
1. Cut the yarn or twine into about forty 12" pieces.
2. Take twenty of these lengths, and tie one end of each to each branch, at ½" interval, to make a loom.
3. Place the loom on a tabletop and stretch the branches apart

to make the yarn or twine taut; tape the branches to the tabletop to maintain the tension.
4. Weave one of the remaining pieces of yarn or twine through the loom, parallel to the branches. Pass it alternately over and under the other pieces of yarn or twine on the loom.
5. Repeat with another length of yarn or twine, but pass it under the pieces you went over before, and over the ones you went under before.
6. Continue to weave the remaining yarn or twine into the loom, alternating the over-and-under pattern.
7. Gently poke the natural items in between the woven yarn or twine.
8. Tie a longer strand of yarn or twine to the ends of one of the branches to make a hanging loop.

Tracking Down Fun

Just as the pioneers of old—and hikers of today—read the trail for signs, your child can learn to read nature's map. Footprints can help your child identify who or what passed a certain spot. Likewise, bent twigs indicate that someone or something has been here. If the broken part of a twig is green inside, it means that this occurred recently. If it's brown and dry, it's an old break and doesn't tell a traveler as much. Bits of cloth or crumbs can also be signs of recent visitors.

ages: 6 years and up
prep time: 15 minutes
skills:
- critical thinking
- using clues

Teach your child to hunt out the signs of visitors to your yard or a park or playground. Add to the challenge by hiding something when she's not looking. Let her observe clues you've left to track down the object.

Rainsticks

Bring a bit of the rain forest into your home. The sounds of the rain coming down through the trees will magically resound from this rainstick. Read the directions with your child as he is ready to do each step.

ages: 6 years and up
prep time: 30 minutes
skills: • listening skills

what you need
- Paper-towel or wrapping-paper tube, about 10" long and no more than 2" in diameter
- Small nail, awl, or other tool to poke toothpick-size holes in tube
- Box of toothpicks
- Quick-setting craft glue
- Kitchen scissors or wire cutters (optional)
- Masking tape
- ½ cup uncooked rice

what to do
1. Starting about 1" from one end of the cardboard tube, pierce two small holes opposite each other through the tube.
2. Continue making pairs of holes, about 1" apart, down the

tube. For best results, rotate the tube slightly before adding each pair of holes, so that the holes create a spiral down the tube.

3. Insert a toothpick through each pair of holes so the toothpick sticks out of both sides.
4. Place a drop of glue on each toothpick at the hole to keep it in place. Snip off the toothpick ends when the glue is dry, and then wrap the tube with masking tape.
5. Place masking tape across one end of the tube, making sure it is completely sealed.
6. Add the rice to the tube and then tape the other end closed.
7. Slowly invert the tube and listen to the peaceful sound of falling rain. Turn it again to continue the sound.

Sun Messages

Hikers often use mirrors to communicate with one another from hill to hill.

ages: 6 years and up
prep time: 2 minutes **skills:** • experimenting with light • creating codes

Your child can make his own sun communicators simply by covering 4" squares of cardboard with aluminum foil. Let him create codes—for instance, one long flash and two short ones could mean, "Is lunch ready?" Encourage him to create a codebook so he and a friend can signal one another wordlessly. Or, introduce him to Morse code and let him spell out his messages.

Natural Math

How far away is an electrical
storm? Kids can find the answer
with careful observations, a watch
with a second hand, and some
math. Here's how:

ages: 6 years and up
skills:
• understanding weather
• math skills

Using a watch, count off the seconds between hearing a clap
of thunder and seeing lightning. The number of seconds indicates how many miles away the storm is. When thunder and
lightning appear simultaneously, the storm is overhead. When
there's a 5-second gap between hearing and seeing, the storm
is 5 miles away.

Older kids who are adept at multiplying and dividing will
enjoy figuring out the warm-weather temperature (when crickets can be heard) using math, too. You'll also need the coop-
eration of a male cricket for this one. Once you've discovered
a place where crickets are chirping, focus your attention on
one insect. (Their chirps are distinguishable if you listen
closely.) Count how many times the cricket chirps within exactly 60 seconds. Subtract 40 from that number. Divide the
remainder by 4. Then add 50 to the number.

For instance:

Number of chirps	100
Subtract 40	60
Divide by 4	15
Add 50	65

The outside temperature is 65°F.

Create a Model-Animal Habitat

Take a bit of the outdoors inside with you. Before beginning this project, help your child research a local animal's habitat, using a book or local park ranger for an information source.

ages: 6 years and up
prep time: 30 minutes
skills:
• observation
• research skills
• manual dexterity

what you need
- Shoebox
- Scissors
- Household items, such as cotton and aluminum foil, to replicate items in nature, such as snow and water
- Outside items, such as sticks, leaves, sand, and pebbles, to replicate other parts of the animal's habitat, such as trees, ground covering, and rocks
- Plastic replica of the animal or a drawing or cutout picture of the animal
- Paint or markers
- Clay or tape

what to do
Make a scene inside the box that reflects what the animal needs to live, including a sleeping place, a source of food, and so forth. Use clay or tape to hold the items upright in the habitat.

Composing

This activity is the ultimate in recycling. You'll probably want to
designate a container inside for
carrying the kitchen scraps out to
your compost site—an empty milk
carton will do the trick. Read the
directions with your child as he is
ready to do each step, and give
him a hand with the wire.

ages: 6 years and up

prep time:
  30 minutes, plus daily
  attention over a few
  weeks

skills:
  • observation
  • recycling

what you need

- Ruler or yardstick
- 4 dowels, each 16" long
- Chicken wire, about 4' × 1'
- Plastic or wire twist-ties
- Black plastic garbage bag
- Clothespins or heavy-duty tape
- Soil from the yard (don't use commercial potting soil)
- Grass clippings, fallen leaves, vegetable scraps, and egg-
  shells
- Water
- Small shovel or spoon

what to do

1. In a sunny part of your yard, mark out a 1' × 1' square on
   the grass or dirt. Insert one end of a dowel into each corner
   of the square.
2. Wrap the chicken wire around the four dowels, making a
   square enclosure. Secure the wire overlap with twist-ties.
   Secure the wire to each dowel with additional twist-ties.

3. Line the walls and floor of the wire enclosure with a black plastic garbage bag, and secure the bag with clothespins or tape.

4. Cut a square of garbage bag slightly larger than the size of the enclosure to form a removable top, and secure it, too, with clothespins or tape.

5. Poke a few holes in the plastic bag on all sides to ensure air flow.

6. Place a few inches of soil in the bottom of the bag. Add some grass clippings, leaves, vegetable scraps, and eggshells. Add some water.

7. Every day or so, remove the top; add some more grass clippings, leaves, vegetable scraps, and eggshells; and stir the mixture with the small shovel. Add more water. Replace the top.

8. After a few weeks, the trash will have evolved into a rich soil—perfect for adding to houseplant pots or the garden.

extra!

You also can put coffee grains and filters, tea bags, and paper towels (unprinted) in your compost. Large uncooked vegetable scraps like broccoli stems should be cut into chunks before composting, or they'll take a really long time to break down. And be sure to never put meat scraps or bones into your compost.

Weather Station

Create your own weather station and never again be at the mercy of professional weather reporters! Do these activities together with your child, letting him do as much as he is able.

ages: 6 years and up
prep time: about 20 minutes per item
skills: • understanding weather

what you need
Weather vane
- Pencil
- 2 pieces of sturdy cardboard, each about 16" square
- Craft knife or scissors
- Clear self-adhesive vinyl covering (optional)
- Tape, white glue, or paste
- Wooden dowel, about 32"

Cloud watcher
- Ruler
- Permanent marker
- Cardboard circle, about 12" in diameter (such as a pizza or cake liner)
- Directional compass
- Small mirror
- Notepad and pencil

Rain gauge
- Ruler
- Permanent marker
- Container with straight sides, such as an empty coffee can

what to do

To make a weather vane. Draw a rooster or any other animal your child fancies on one piece of cardboard, cut it out, and use it as a pattern to cut an identical shape from the other piece. (If you want your weather vane to be weatherproof, cover one side of each piece of cardboard with clear self-adhesive vinyl before you draw and cut out the shapes; be sure to reverse the first shape when using it as a pattern.) Tape or glue the two cutouts together around the edges, leaving a 1" opening on the bottom. (If you've used the vinyl, use additional strips of it to secure the two shapes.) Slip the wooden dowel through the opening. Insert the dowel in the ground or elsewhere out in the open, perhaps attached to a fence, so the cutout critter spins freely when the wind blows.

To make a cloud watcher. Use the ruler and marker to divide the cardboard circle into quadrants. Then, referring to the compass, mark the outer rim of the cardboard circle with the directional points of the compass. Place the circle and the compass on the ground or an outdoor table. Position the compass so the arrow points north, and then align the north mark on the circle with north on the compass. To complete the cloud watcher, place the mirror in the middle of the circle. Now look down at the mirror and watch which way the clouds are passing. Record your information.

To make a rain gauge. Using the ruler and starting from the bottom, mark the inside of a straight-sided container, such as a coffee can, at ½" increments. Place the container outside, away from the side of the house and other obstructions. After a rain, check to see how many inches of rain fell.

Shell Candles

This activity helps your child pre-
serve the unique shapes of shells
as pretty candles.

what you need
- Shoebox or other sturdy box
- Wet sand, enough to fill the box
- Large seashell
- String, cut into 8" lengths
- Pencils
- Paraffin or candle stubs
- Electric skillet

ages: 7 years and up
prep time: 1 hour, plus waiting time
skills: • appreciation of nature • understanding the properties of wax

what to do
1. Have your child fill the box with the wet sand. Then have him press the seashell into the sand to create a deep impression, and remove it carefully. Have him make as many impressions as he likes, spacing them a few inches apart.
2. Have your child tie one end of each string around the middle of a pencil to form a wick, and press the other end into the middle of a sand impression, burying it just a little. He can roll any excess wick onto the pencil and rest the pencil across the top of the box.
3. Melt the wax in the electric skillet and pour it into the impression(s), keeping each wick straight.
4. Wait for the wax to harden (about 2 hours) and let your child dig out the candle(s). Wipe away excess sand to reveal the seashell shape. To harden the candle(s) further, dip into cold water for 1 to 2 seconds.

PARENTS ALERT

When it comes to melted paraffin or any other wax, adults must always supervise. Wax is extremely flammable and should never be melted in a saucepan (even in a double boiler) on a stove top.

Sundial

Learning to read a clock can become even more meaningful when done with a little help from nature. Try this on a sunny day:

ages: 7 years and up

prep time:
about 30 minutes

skills:
- understanding time
- relationship of clocks to sundials

what you need
- Drafting compass or protractor and ruler
- Marker
- Cardboard circle, 12" in diameter
- Clock with clearly marked numerals
- Cardboard triangle, 6" at the base and 3" high
- Heavy-duty tape

what to do
1. Divide and mark the perimeter of the cardboard circle into 12 equal sections.

2. Ask your child to number the marks to indicate the hours, using a clock as a guide.

3. Have your child set the triangle upright on the circle, placing the sharp point in the center and aligning the blade with the 12 o'clock mark; then have her tape the triangle in place.

4. As the time approaches any daytime hour, she should place the sundial outdoors on a level, sunny spot. On the hour exactly, have her orient the sundial so that the shadow cast shows exactly that time of day.

5. Your child can then check the sundial every hour to see how the sun casts its shadow to show the time. (At noon, there will be no shadow.)

out and about

places to go and things to do on the way

You don't have to travel far to expand your child's understanding of the world. Neighborhood jaunts, in fact, provide a universe of stimulation and meaning for your child.

In this section you'll get ideas for taking a new, fresher look at sites right outside your door. You'll also find a host of ideas for planning trips with an educational slant, new ways to celebrate each season, and lots of boredom busters for when you're traveling.

out and about

Put these items in a backpack to keep in the car or carry with you on trains, planes, or buses to entertain and soothe kids on the way.

- Plastic bottle filled with fresh water
- Deck of playing cards or pictures
- Book
- Tape recorder and some story or song tapes
- Comfy pillow or stuffed animal
- Drawing tablet and chunky crayons
- Silent, handheld electronic or mechanical game
- Hand puppet
- Wipes for cleaning up messes and for feeling refreshed
- Fresh T-shirt to change into for cool comfort
- Unbreakable, handheld mirror
- Small metal "slate" (such as a cookie tin) and magnetic letters or words

Springtime Day Trips

Make springtime walks and other neighborhood outings special this season. Here's how:

ages: all ages	
location: close to home	

- Bring along seeds to feed the birds.
- Photograph or draw a favorite scene.
- Scout for all signs of new blooming plants.
- Listen to a tape of classical music.
- Break out a new box of sidewalk chalk.
- Go out right after a rain and search for rainbows.
- Take advantage of mild evening temperatures and longer days by heading outside after dinner.
- Look for a robin, caterpillar, or returning geese.
- Find a gently sloping hill to roll down.
- Listen for birdsongs. Try recording some and replaying the tape at home.
- Wash your bike while your child washes hers.
- Plant flowers or bulbs either in a backyard garden or window box.
- Have an egg hunt.

extra!

Take a photo of your child standing in front of a familiar spot that clearly shows springtime. Return to the same spot once each season, taking a new picture each time. At the end of a year, you'll have a frame-worthy collection.

Summer Days and Evenings

Try the following cool alternatives to indoor air-conditioned fun:

ages: all ages	
location: close to home	

- Give your child an outdoor hose shower in his bathing suit instead of an evening bath.
- Read under a shady tree.
- With older kids, share frozen banana-pop treats (put a craft stick into a banana, wrap in wax paper, and freeze).
- Slurp homemade snowcones (fill a cup almost to the top with shaved ice, add fruit juice, and stick in a straw).
- Plan and carry out a tricycle/bicycle brigade parade on Independence Day. All you need to do is line up your child with some of her friends on their vehicles, attach a flag to each handlebar, and play appropriate Sousa marches on a portable tape player. Then lead the group around for the enjoyment of the entire neighborhood.
- Collect a pail of shells at the beach.
- Catch fireflies and let them go.
- Tell one another what you see in the clouds.
- Hunt for crickets.
- Practice skimming stones across a pond.

Autumn Activities

When autumn leaves begin to fall, head outdoors and try these:

| **ages:** all ages |
| **location:** close to home |

* Catch a leaf before it hits the ground.
* Collect newly fallen leaves and use them to decorate your front door. Or simply tape them to a sheet of poster board and admire them indoors, again and again.
* Listen for geese heading south.
* Count school buses.
* Gather a great big pile of leaves and jump in it.
* Hang a windsock.
* Draw with chalk on the sidewalk.
* Visit a farm (if you're a city dweller) or visit the city (if you're a country mouse).
* Pick apples.
* Choose the best pumpkin and decorate it.
* Collect pinecones.
* Have an "Indian summer" picnic.
* Rent a tandem bicycle and cycle together.

Winter Fun

If winter threatens to keep you indoors, think of these possibilities
before heading for the couch:

ages: all ages
location: close to home

- Make snow angels.
- Visit a Christmas tree farm.
- Catch snowflakes on your tongues.
- Hang a bird feeder.
- Drink hot chocolate on a park bench.
- Visit the beach to see how it looks in winter.
- Take a tour of neighborhood holiday decorations.
- Bring homemade cookies to a housebound neighbor.
- Spray-paint the snow (fill a spray bottle with water mixed
  with a little food coloring).
- Hang sleighbells from trees and bushes.
- Build and dress a snow family.
- Play tic-tac-toe—or catch—in the snow.
- Collect natural objects to add to your door wreath.

Find Habitats

Who—and what—shares your neighborhood?

ages: all ages
location: close to home

Go on a hunt with your child to find the habitats and homes of various animals—birds in nests, ants in anthills, squirrels in trees, fish in lakes.

Backseat Travel Tips

From the confines of her car seat, your child can be entertained in a variety of ways. Consider these ideas to cut down on backseat boredom.

ages: babies and tod- dlers
location: car

Tape a favorite story. In addition to commercially prepared story tapes, those in which you do the reading make for especially nice moments for your child. Just put them in the car tape player.

Post a photo. As an alternative to staring at the back of your head for the trip, tape a smiling photo of yourself and your child to the back of the front seat. It's wonderfully reassuring, especially to a young child who can't figure out why you've turned your back on him.

Select some active, but quiet, amusements. Good backseat toys for babies include seat-attached busy boxes and chew toys (attached to the seat with plastic chains for easy retrieval). For older kids, the list includes slates with chunky chalks, Slinkies (great for just slinking from hand to hand), and books and crayons. Store them in a kid-size suitcase in the car.

New Ways to Travel

In our highly specialized world, where there's a vehicle for just about every road condition, show your child that with a little imagination, getting from here to there can be done with flair.

ages: babies and toddlers	
location: outdoors	

Use a sled on the beach. Plastic-bottomed sleds glide easily across the sand. They have the added benefit of providing a handy transport for all your beach gear from the parking lot to the shoreline.

Decorate a trike. Streamers, stickers, and a homemade or store-bought license plate turn an ordinary trike into a high-end model. Just be sure that anything you tie on can't get caught in the wheels or pedals.

Opt for a wagon. The constraints of a stroller can get boring after a while for your toddler. On close-to-home trips, let your child spread his legs and pile in his toys for a ride in a high-sided wagon. It gives him a fun, new perspective.

Add a steering wheel. If yours is a take-charge kind of toddler, consider attaching a busy-box steering wheel (available in most toy stores) to the front of her stroller. It gives her a great feeling of being in charge of the destination.

Dress for your backpack rider. If your child is a regular back-pack rider, the top of your head has become very familiar terrain. Spruce up the scenery with a silly hat: Draw a happy face on a light-colored baseball cap or wear a cap with a built-in pinwheel.

See the world on skates. Holding your older toddler's hand firmly, take a tour around the block with your child on skates. He'll study the sidewalk as never before!

Make Friends at the Firehouse

Most kids are drawn to the brightly colored trucks and the friendly welcome they're likely to receive at their local firehouse. So the next time you pass a firehouse, knock

ages: toddlers and pre-schoolers
location: your local firehouse

on the door and ask if this is a good time for a tour.

Many fire departments allow children to get a close-up look at the trucks, try on the firefighters' hats and boots, and even turn on the siren on the truck. Just be prepared for a sudden (and loud) ending to your excursion if duty should call.

Before your adventure, read a picture book about firefighters.

Shopping-Cart Search

From his perch in the shopping cart, your child has a great view of the wonders of the supermarket. Try these observation games the next time you're aisle-hopping.

ages: toddlers and pre-schoolers
location: supermarket

Pick a color. Ask your toddler how many red things he can find in the produce department. What about yellow? Can he find anything purple?

What size? Look at the small, medium, and family-size packages of various items and let your toddler tell you which one is biggest and which one is smallest.

Read the pictures. Show your child various packaged goods and let her identify what's inside by looking at the box.

Chill out. Let your child touch things in the frozen-food bins, and encourage him to think about which foods in your home are also kept cold.

Match the coupon. Hand your child a coupon for a particular item and, when you reach that aisle, invite her to find the item.

Watch the fish. Few toddlers can resist spending a few moments observing the lobster tank and the fresh fish department.

Find favorites. If your family usually buys a particular brand of a common item, such as boxed cereal, ask your toddler to find "our special cereal."

Wagon-Train Tour

Have your child load up her wagon or doll carriage and give her toys a tour of the neighborhood.

ages: 24 months and up	
location: outdoors	

What sights can she name and describe? What does she like (or not like) about each place? What are her favorite places?

Take notes as you go and when you get back home, you can create a little book with your child's words for her to illustrate.

Special Delivery

Shopping can be a bit tedious for a toddler. Seeing the goods delivered, however, can be pure fun, especially for the truck lovers in your family.

ages: 24 months and up	
location: delivery areas of stores	

Check out the back doors of various stores and watch the goods being delivered. The conveyor belts are especially interesting.

See Spot

You'll need a camera for this activity, preferably an instant one.

ages: 24 months and up

location: outdoors or in

Take photos of various scenes and objects around the neighborhood. Give our child the pictures and have him match the picture to the place where it was taken as you take your stroll past those locations.

---

extra!

For added fun, take a separate picture of him standing at each location. (Or, just get duplicates of the photos. But having one picture with the child in it and one without is more fun.) Then you've got a deck of matching cards for a game of memory:

1. Turn all of the photos face down, in neat rows. (It will be difficult for a toddler to play with more than six cards, or three matched pairs, at a time.)

2. Ask your child to turn over two photos, one at a time. If the cards match (i.e., if they're pictures of the same location), he puts the cards in his winning pile and gets to go again. If the location photos are different, he turns both back over, trying to remember where each one is in its row. You should take a turn and do the same.

---

extra! *(continued)*

3. For his next turn, he turns over two more photos, again trying to match the second to the first.

At first, he'll have to guess to find a match, but after several
turns, your child will have a good idea about where many of
the photos are. The game is over when he's matched every pair.

Museum Match-Up

Museums provide a wealth of
stimulation for children. Help
yours focus her attention.

ages: 3 years and up
location:
museums

For this activity, start at the gift
shop and purchase a few postcards that illustrate some of the
exhibits you're about to see. As you take your tour with your
child, help her hunt down the items on her cards.

Tip When visiting museums with young children, be aware of
signs of fatigue and make your exit before the experience
becomes overwhelming for your child.

Storefront Search

From pizza and doughnut makers to shoe and car repairers, there are bound to be some local merchants who can give your child a close-up look at what's going on.

ages: 3 years and up
location:
  local stores

Stop by places where you know the merchant and arrange a convenient time for a personal tour. Point out to your child the processes involved in each place of business. And, if you're observing food preparations, be sure to sample the end product with your child.

Take a Silly Sojourn

There's no need to be too serious about your outdoor adventures. Add some fun by:

ages: 3 years and up
location:
  outdoors

- Walking backwards while whistling or singing a song
- Avoiding all cracks in the sidewalk
- Seeing how far you can kick a small stone or a tin can
- Hopping on one foot or skipping
- Leaving a trail of bread crumbs for a squirrel or bird to follow

- Rolling a hula hoop as you go
- Counting people wearing purple (or with another distinguishing feature)
- Seeing how long you can go without giggling

Are We There Yet?

Improve your child's counting skills while making the last minutes of a trip more fun.

| ages: 3 years and up |
| location: |
| car |

When you are about a minute away from home, ask your child how long it will take to get there, counting out each second. Encourage him to guess and then start counting. Count by ones in the beginning and as he masters this, try counting by twos, fives, and tens.

For a variation, use a nonstandard measurement, asking, for instance, how many times he can sing a favorite song verse before you pull into the driveway.

Expand the View

Use special lenses to get a close-up view of things your pre-schooler might miss unaided.

ages: 3 years and up	
location: outdoors	

Demonstrate using binoculars to make scenes appear closer or farther away, a magnifying glass to home in on ants in the grass (take care to not hurt the ants by beaming concentrated sunlight on them), or a telescope to view the night sky.

Backseat Bingo

Your own variations of this perennial favorite will challenge your child's observation skills while traveling. Any game of backseat

ages: 4 years and up	
location: car	

bingo can be played alone or in competition with other players. For all versions, begin with 25 magazine pictures or drawings, each about 1½" square, of items that are likely to be spotted from the car window. If more than one person is playing, make a photocopy of the cutouts or draw an additional set. Then enjoy one or more of these versions:

Quick pix. For each player, make a game board with a transparent 35mm slide page, available at most photo shops. Simply insert the pictures, one per slot, in a five-by-five grid. A player marks his sightings with a grease pencil. For additional games, erase the markings with a tissue, and rearrange the pictures in the slots.

Multiple choice. For this, you'll need access to a photocopy machine. First, draw a five-by-five grid on a sheet of plain white paper, with squares big enough to hold your cutout pictures or drawings. Arrange the 25 cutouts or drawings in the grids, holding them in place with small pieces of tape. Make one copy; rearrange the position of about five of the cutouts or drawings and make another copy. Keep rearranging some of the items and making enough copies for players to play multiple games on long trips. Give each player a clipboard to hold her game board and a crayon for marking off sightings.

---

extra!

You can make reusable game boards for "multiple choice." Before distributing the game boards, cover each one with clear self-adhesive vinyl. Players can make sightings with grease pencils.

Right and Left/ North and South

Which direction are you traveling?

ages: 4 years and up
location: car

When you're doing some local driving with your child, have him announce which direction you've gone with each turn. For older kids, have them use highway signs or the position of the sun to determine if you're traveling north, south, east, or west.

A Playground Alphabet

On your next playground visit, help your child identify objects, attributes, and actions that begin with each letter of the alphabet. For instance:

ages: 4 years and up
location: neighborhood

Apples
Bench
Curb
Dog

Electric light
flowers
Game board
Hat

Ice-cream truck	Runner
Jungle gym	Sand
Kite	Truck
Lawn	Upside-down kid
Music	Voices
Newspaper	Water
Orange (the fruit or the color)	X-ray
Pail	Yellow
Quick kid	Zipper

A Three-Sense Tour

Enhance your child's senses by fo-
cusing on one at a time.

ages: 4 years and up
location:
outdoors

Encourage your child to close her
eyes during a walk. In a safe,
enclosed area, ask if she'd like to be blindfolded for this special "sensory tour." Walk slowly, helping her identify the
sounds she hears. Guide her to a familiar thing, such as a tree
trunk, and let her identify it by touch alone. Place a flower
under her nose. Does the smell help her know what you're
holding?

Take an Art Break

When you're walking on the beach or in a snowy area, take a break and create some art. All you need is a cookie sheet or colored paper, a few small stones, and a little breeze.

ages: 4 years and up	
location:	a sandy or snowy area

Place the cookie sheet or paper on the ground, and strategically arrange the stones. Sprinkle some sand or powdery snow on top of the cookie sheet or paper (or simply let nature blow some your way). Then just watch as the breeze rearranges the sand or snow in swirls around the stones. The everchanging results are simply beautiful to behold.

You can also set your cookie sheet or paper and stones in the backyard sandbox or on an outdoor table on a snowy day, where you can revisit the spot often and observe the changed designs.

Rearview Mirror

You use your rearview and side-view mirrors all the time. Why not let your child get a good look at what's behind her on the road, too?

ages: 4 years and up	
location:	car

All you need is a pocket mirror for your child to position in such a way as to check out the just-passed scenery. Remind her, of course, to keep her hands and the mirror inside the car window. (It's best to do this activity at a time of day—neither sunrise or sunset—when she's not likely to catch the sun's reflection in her mirror, which could distract other drivers.)

Counting Categories

Have each passenger pick a color and count as many cars of that color as he sees on the road. The first player to reach a predetermined number—say 5 for the younger players and 20 for older kids—is the winner.

ages: 4 years and up

location:
  car

---

extra!

For kids who've become adept at counting colored cars, let them pick a more challenging category that might be seen—and counted—on a journey. For instance, kids can count motorcycles, farm animals, roadside produce stands, cars with the number 4 in the license plate, or cars with bicycles hooked to the rear or on top.

Adopt a Tree

At home, there are special places that belong to your child—her bed, a favorite chair, a playroom.

ages:	4 years and up
location:	outdoors, close to home

Outside, there can be spaces and objects that offer the comfort of familiarity, too. A tree, especially, is a wonderful thing to call one's own, even if it's in a city park. The important thing is to claim it, care for it, and visit it regularly.

When your child is old enough to choose, let her pick "her" tree. Take a photo or have her draw a picture of it to display at home. Encourage her to tell her friends and family members about her tree. Help your child study it: What does the bark feel like? What shape are its leaves or needles? Collect fallen leaves or needles. Water it. Read stories under it and make up stories about it.

A Big Yellow Dot

Colors and shapes aren't found only where you expect them. Help your child learn to appreciate everything around her.

ages:	4 years and up
location:	outdoors and in

There's no telling where your child might find a big yellow dot. Have your child look all around to find them—in the sky (the sun), on the road (a yield light), in the garden (a daisy's center), at home (on polka-dotted clothing or in a sunny-side-up egg.) To keep count of her finds, cut out ten or more yellow circles from construction paper and hand her a circle for each one she discovers.

---

extra!

Make several drawings—a landscape, a flower, a traffic light, and even a bird's-eye view of a fried egg—leaving out the yellow circle. Have your child paste a yellow dot on each, wherever she thinks it should go.

READING TIE-INS

Ten Black Dots
by Donald Crews (Mulberry Books)

Yellow and You
by Candace Whitman (Abbeville Press)

Make Your Own Postcards

You can buy commercially produced postcard kits at most photo stores or make your own using inexpensive store-bought postcards, your own photos, and some paste.

| **ages:** 5 years and up |
| **location:**
  away from home |

On a day during your travels when you'll be in one location for a few hours, drop off the film that you've shot so far on your trip for 1-hour developing. (Ask that the photo be sized 3" × 5" or 4" × 6" to match the size of your purchased or precut postcards.) Choose some shots of your child at a favorite location and paste the photo onto the card. When the paste is dry and the picture well secured, write your message and address and mail it as usual.

Another fun way to enhance store-bought cards is to add cutout pictures of your child to a fabulous postcard scene. Just be sure the cutout is securely attached before mailing.

Mystery Tour

This activity requires a bit of preplanning.

| **ages:** 5 years and up |
| **location:**
  in the car or on foot |

Collect some clues about the place you're going to see, but don't tell the other players. Along the way, dole out the clues. For instance, for a drive to the beach, give your child an egg timer (the sand-filled kind) and say, "Our destination has something to do with this clue." Give each player one guess. If the destination isn't guessed, hand out another clue, such as a whiff of suntan lotion that you've dabbed onto a tissue. Depending on the age of your child, make the clues easier or more difficult.

Beat the Clock

There's no end to the variations on this car game.

ages: 5 years and up
location: car

For the most fun, play this a few minutes before reaching a toll booth, exit, or other destination. Have each player choose a thing, number, or color. Then the first one who spots that attribute on another car or road sign (for example, a 5 in a license plate or on a speed-limit sign, or red on a car or road sign) before reaching that destination, wins.

---

extra!

You can play this game using the radio, too. In this version, players can choose any word (as long as they each choose a different word). Then they listen carefully to the radio for that word in a song, news report, or ad within a set time limit.

The Traveling Band Is a . . .

Challenge your children's creativity while helping them practice the alphabet.

ages: 5 years and up
location: car

This alphabet game can go on for hours. Beginning with the letter *a*, each player describes the traveling band's adventures: "The traveling band is an awesome band. They went to Alaska and ate apricots."

The next player does *b*. By the time they reach *z*, your kids may be saying, "The traveling band is a zany band. They went to the zoo and zoomed in on a zebra."

The Traveling Band Is a . . . #2

In this version, each player adds an activity that the next player repeats before adding her own activity to the story of the traveling band. Besides being just plain

ages: 5 years and up
location: car

fun, this game sharpens memory skills and creativity. Here's how it might work with two players:

Player 1: The traveling band had an old jalopy.

Player 2: The traveling band had an old jalopy and a red biplane.

Player 1: The traveling band had an old jalopy, a red biplane, and a horse named Pete.

Player 2: The traveling band had an old jalopy, a red biplane, a horse named Pete, and a silly kazoo player.

Well, you get the idea.

Start a Road Collection

Kids are born consumers, but this game can keep the "gimmees" to a minimum.

ages: 5 years and up	
location: away from home	

Before setting out on a trip, choose an item that your child can collect at each stop, ranging from free things (leaves, pebbles, dinner napkins) to moderately priced goods (T-shirts, caps, badges), so that by the end of the trip your child will have an array of similar souvenirs. He can start a collection, and you can avoid arguments.

License-Plate Watch

License-plate-watching inspires a
number of car games:

ages: 5 years and up
location: car

A to Z. Find the alphabet on license plates. The trick is to find
the letters in order—*AZK* on the first plate spotted counts only
as *A*; the kids must find *B* next.

1 to 9. This is the number version of *A* to *Z*, in which kids
spot the numbers *1* through *9*.

What state? How many different state plates can you find?

Mottoes. Record the mottoes or other descriptors on different
state plates. Then have your child consider why Florida's tag
bears the phrase "The Sunshine State" or why New Hampshire
opts for "Live Free or Die."

Menu Musings

If your trips take you outside your
region to places that serve up local specials, menu scanning can
be fun and informative.

ages: 6 years and up
location: restaurants

The more adventurous child might like to sample some local cuisine. Yours may prefer simply finding out why it's special to the area, what it looks like, and so on. Keep a running list of foods that you find on your travels but not in your own locale.

Autograph Hounds

This is a twist on the common practice of guests signing in at landmark houses and adding a comment or two about their visit.

ages: 7 years and up
location: anywhere

Have your child carry a "guest book" on your travels and encourage him to collect signatures and comments from people you meet along the way. For instance, a park ranger can sign in by noting something special about your campsite; in a city, a hotel clerk can sign in by telling some local lore. Kids can collect drawings done by fellow young travelers, stickers, and other mementos.

Compound-Word Tour

See how many compound-word sights and objects you and your child can find on your travels.

| **ages:** 7 years and up |
| **location:**
  in a car or on foot |

You might see, for example, an airport, a riverbank, a houseboat, a lighthouse, a playground, an overpass, amd a highway. The possibilities are endless.

I Spy an Airplane

Here's a spelling and storytelling game that can shorten any road trip.

| **ages:** 7 years and up |
| **location:**
  car |

To start, one player finds something that begins with *A*, spells it, and creates a story line that incorporates each letter. Here's how it might go:

I spy an airplane. **A-I-R-P-L-A-N-E**

Alice flew on it.

I joined her.

Ronnie met us.

People sat in rows.

Lunch was served.

Afterwards, we watched a movie.

Nobody liked it.

Except for me!

Younger players might choose shorter words to keep their spelling and storytelling tasks a bit easier. For example:

I spy an ant. **A-N-T.**

Ants like picnics.

No one invites them.

They come anyway.

Add It Up

This game hones the ability to do mental math.

ages: 7 years and up	
location:	
car	

Players work toward adding single-digit numbers to reach the goal of 100. The first player says any number from 1 to 10. The next player adds a number that is more or less than the number stated (to ensure that players don't simply add 10 at each turn).

For example, if the first player says, "9," the second player might say, "9 plus 2 is 11." The next player then says, "11 plus 5 is 16." Players keep going until the last player—and winner—provides a number that leads to a sum of 100.

Plan a Trip

Kids are used to being passive when it comes to travel planning. But joining in on the planning stages offers practice in a host of skills. Here are some ways your child can help:

| ages: 7 years and up |
| location:
  home |

- Write to the tourist board requesting brochures.
- Review a map to find the shortest routes between stops.
- Prepare a packing list for his own belongings.
- Schedule an entire day.
- Write a budget for a portion of the trip—perhaps how he's planning to use his own spending money.
- Research a particular attraction or area you'll be visiting.
- Go on the Internet to find out more about your destination.

Index